Apu Ollantay

Sir Clements R. Markham

To my friend,
therapist, mentor
Linda Domenitz

From David
Bravo.

Table of Contents

Apu Ollantay

Sir Clements R. Markham

Kessinger Publishing reprints thousands of hard–to–find books!

Apu Ollantay
        A Drama of the Time of the Incas

APU OLLANTAY

A DRAMA OF THE TIME OF THE INCAS

SOVEREIGNS OF PERU

ABOUT A.D. 1470

FIRST REDUCED TO WRITING BY DR. VALDEZ, CUBA OF SICUANI A.D. 1770

THE ORIGINAL MANUSCRIPT COPIED BY DR. JUSTO PASTOR JUSTINIANI

THIS JUSTINIANI TEXT COPIED AT LARIS, IN APRIL 1863, BY CLEMENTS R. MARKHAM

A FREE TRANSLATION INTO ENGLISH BY SIR CLEMENTS MARKHAM, K.C.B. [1910]

INTRODUCTION

The drama was cultivated by the Incas, and dramatic performances were enacted before them. Garcilasso de la Vega, Molina, and Salcamayhua are the authorities who received and have recorded the information given by the Amautas respecting the Inca drama. Some of these dramas, and portions of others, were preserved in the memories of members of Inca and Amauta families. The Spanish priests, especially the Jesuits of Juli, soon discovered the dramatic aptitude of the people. Plays were composed and acted, under priestly auspices, which contained songs and other fragments of the ancient Inca drama. These plays were called 'Autos Sacramentales.'

But complete Inca dramas were also preserved in the memories of members of the Amauta caste and, until the rebellion of 1781, they were acted. The drama of Ollantay was first reduced to writing and arranged for acting by Dr. Don Antonio Valdez, the Cura of Tinto. It was acted before his friend Jose Gabriel Condorcanqui[FN#1] in about 1775. Taking the name of his maternal ancestor, the Inca Tupac Amaru, the ill–fated Condorcanqui rose in rebellion, was defeated, taken, and put to death under torture, in the great square of Cuzco. In the monstrous sentence 'the representation of dramas as well as all other festivals which the Indians celebrate in memory of their Incas' was prohibited.[FN#2] This is a clear proof that before 1781 these Quichua dramas were acted.

[FN#1] INCA–PACHACUTI

|

TUPAC YUPANQUI

|

INCA HUAYNA CCAPAC

|

MANCO INCA

|

TUPAC AMARU

|

JUANA NUSTA = DIEGO CONDORCANQUI

|

FELIPE CONDORCANQUI

|

PEDRO CONDORCANQUI

|

MIGUEL CONDORCANQUI

|

JOSE GABRIEL CONDORCANQUI (TUPAC AMARU)

[FN#2] 'Sentencia pronunciada en el Cuzco por el Visitador Don Jose Antonio de Areche, contra Jose Gabriel Tupac Amaru.' In Coleccion de obras y documentos de Don Pedro de Angelis, vol. V. (Buenos Ayres, 1836– 7).

The original manuscript of Valdez was copied by his friend Don Justo Pastor Justiniani, and this copy was inherited by his son. There was another copy in the convent of San Domingo at Cuzco, but it is corrupt, and there are several omissions and mistakes of a copyist. Dr. Valdez died, at a very advanced age, in 1816. In 1853 the original manuscript was in the possession of his nephew and heir, Don Narciso Cuentas of Tinta.

The Justiniani copy was, in 1853, in the possession of Dr. Don Pablo Justiniani, Cura of Laris, and son of Don Justo Pastor Justiniani. He is a descendant of the Incas.[FN#3] In April 1853 I went to Laris, a secluded valley of the Andes, and made a careful copy of the drama of Ollantay. From this Justiniani text my first very faulty line–for–line translation was made in 1871, as well as the present free translation.

[FN#3] INCA PACHACUTI.
|
TUPAC YUPANQUI
|
HUAYNA CCAPAC
|
MANCO INCA
|
MARIA TUPAC USCA = PEDRO ORTIZ DE ORUE
|
CATALINA ORTIZ =LUIS JUSTINIANI
|
LUIS JUSTINIANI
|
LUIS JUSTINIANI
|
NICOLO JUSTINIANI
|
JUSTO PASTOR JUSTINIANI
|
Dr. PABLO POLICARPO JUSTINIANI(Cura of Laris)

The first printed notice of Ollantay appeared in the Museo Erudito, Nos. 5 to 9, published at Cuzco in 1837, and edited by Don Jose Palacios. The next account of the drama, with extracts, was in the 'Antiguedades Peruanas,' a work published in 1851 jointly by Dr. von Tschudi and Don Mariaiao Rivero of Arequipa. The complete text, from the copy in the convent of San Domingo at Cuzco, was first published at Vienna in 1853 by Dr. von

Tschudi in his 'Die Kechua Sprache. It was obtained for him by Dr. Ruggendas of Munich. The manuscript was a corrupt version, and in very bad condition, in parts illegible from damp. In 1868 Don Jose Barranca published a Spanish translation, from the Dominican text of von Tschudi. The learned Swiss naturalist, von Tschudi, published a revised edition of his translation at Vienna in 1875, with a parallel German translation. In 1871 I printed the Justiniani text with a literal, line–for–line translation, but with many mistakes, since corrected; and in 1874, a Peruvian, Don Jose Fernandez Nodal, published the Quichua text with a Spanish translation.

In 1878 Gavino Pacheco Zegarra published his version of Ollantay, with a free translation in French. His text is a manuscript of the drama which he found in his uncle's library. Zegarra, as a native of Peru whose language was Quichua, had great advantages. He was a very severe, and often unfair, critic of his predecessors.

The work of Zegarra is, however, exceedingly valuable. He was not only a Quichua scholar, but also accomplished and well read. His notes on special words and on the construction of sentences are often very interesting. But his conclusions respecting several passages which are in the Justiniani text, but not in the others, are certainly erroneous. Thus he entirely spoils the dialogue between the Uillac Uma and Piqui Chaqui by omitting the humorous part contained in the Justiniani text; and makes other similar omissions merely because the passages are not in his text. Zegarra gives a useful vocabulary at the end of all the words which occur in the drama.

The great drawback to the study of Zegarra's work is that he invented a number of letters to express the various modifications of sound as they appealed to his ear. No one else can use them, while they render the reading of his own works difficult and intolerably tiresome.

The last publication of a text of Ollantay was by the Rev. J. H. Gybbon Spilsbury, at Buenos Ayres in 1907, accompanied by Spanish, English, and French translations in parallel columns.

There is truth in what Zegarra says, that the attempts to translate line for line, by von Tschudi and myself, 'fail to convey a proper idea of the original drama to European readers, the result being alike contrary to the genius of the modern languages of Europe and to that of the Quichua language.' Zegarra accordingly gives a very free translation in

Apu Ollantay

French.

In the present translation I believe that I have always preserved the sense of the original, without necessarily binding myself to the words. The original is in octosyllabic lines. Songs and important speeches are in quatrains of octosyllabic lines, the first and last rhyming, and the second and third. I have endeavoured to keep to octosyllabic lines as far as possible, because they give a better idea of the original; and I have also tried to preserve the form of the songs and speeches.

The drama opens towards the close of the reign of the Inca Pachacuti, the greatest of all the Incas, and the scene is laid at Cuzco or at Ollantay–tampu, in the valley of the Vilcamayu. The story turns on the love of a great chief, but not of the blood–royal, with a daughter of the Inca. This would not have been prohibited in former reigns, for the marriage of a sister by the sovereign or his heir, and the marriage of princesses only with princes of the blood–royal, were rules first introduced by Pachacuti.[FN#4] His imperial power and greatness led him to endeavour to raise the royal family far above all others.

[FN#4] The wives of the Incas were called ccoya. The ccoya of the second Inca was a daughter of the chief of Sanoc. The third Inca married a daughter of the chief of Oma, the fourth married a girl of Tacucaray, the wife of the fifth was a daughter of a Cuzco chief. The sixth Inca married a daughter of the chief of Huayllacan, the seventh married a daughter of the chief of Ayamarca, and the eighth went to Anta for a wife. This Anta lady was the mother of Pachacuti. The wife of Pachacuti, named Anahuarqui, was a daughter of the chief of Choco. There was no rule about marrying sisters when Pachacuti succeeded. He introduced it by making his son Tupac Yupanqui marry his daughter Mama Ocllo, but this was quite unprecedented. The transgression of a rule which he had just made may account for his extreme severity.

The play opens with a dialogue between Ollantay and Piqui Chaqui, his page, a witty and humorous lad. Ollantay talks of his love for the Princess Cusi Coyllur, and wants Piqui Chaqui to take a message to her, while the page dwells on the danger of loving in such a quarter, and evades the question of taking a message. Then to them enters the Uillac Uma, or High Priest of the Sun, who remonstrates with Ollantay—a scene of great solemnity, and very effective.

6

Apu Ollantay

The next scene is in the Queen's palace. Anahuarqui, the Queen, is discovered with the Princess Cusi Coyllur, who bitterly laments the absence of Ollantay. To them enters the Inca Pachacuti, quite ignorant that his daughter has not only married Ollantay in secret, but that she is actually with child by him. Her mother keeps her secret. The Inca indulges in extravagant expressions of love for his daughter. Then boys and girls enter dancing and singing a harvest song. Another very melancholy yarahui is sung; both capable of being turned by the Princess into presages of the fate of herself and her husband.

In the third scene Ollantay prefers his suit to the Inca Pachacuti in octosyllabic quatrains, the first and last lines rhyming, and the second and third. His suit is rejected with scorn and contempt. Ollantay next appears on the heights above Cuzco. In a soliloquy he declares himself the implacable enemy of Cuzco and the Inca. Then Piqui Chaqui arrives with the news that the Queen's palace is empty, and abandoned, and that Cusi Coyllur has quite disappeared; while search is being made for Ollantay. While they are together a song is sung behind some rocks, in praise of Cusi Coyllur's beauty. Then the sound of clarions and people approaching is heard, and Ollantay and Piqui Chaqui take to flight. The next scene finds the Inca enraged at the escape of Ollantay, and ordering his general Rumi−naui to march at once, and make him prisoner. To them enters a chasqui, or messenger, bringing the news that Ollantay has collected a great army at Ollantay−tampu, and that the rebels have proclaimed him Inca.

The second act opens with a grand scene in the hall of the fortress−palace of Ollantay−tampu. Ollantay is proclaimed Inca by the people, and he appoints the Mountain Chief, Urco Huaranca, general of his army. Urco Huaranca explains the dispositions he has made to oppose the army advancing from Cuzco, and his plan of defence. In the next scene Rumi−naui, as a fugitive in the mountains, describes his defeat and the complete success of the strategy of Ollantay and Urco Huaranca. His soliloquy is in the octosyllabic quatrains. The last scene of the second act is in the gardens of the Convent of Virgins of the Sun. A young girl is standing by a gate which opens on the street. This, as afterwards appears, is Yma Sumac, the daughter of Ollantay and Cusi Coyllur, aged ten, but ignorant of her parentage. To her enters Pitu Salla, an attendant, who chides her for being so fond of looking out at the gate. The conversation which follows shows that Yma Sumac detests the convent and refuses to take the vows. She also has heard the moans of some sufferer, and importunes Pitu Salla to tell her who it is. Yma Sumac goes as Mama Ccacca enters and cross examines Pitu Salla on her progress in persuading Yma Sumac to adopt convent life. This Mama Ccacca is one of the Matrons or Mama Cuna, and she is also the jailer of Cusi Coyllur.

The third act opens with an amusing scene between the Uillac Uma and Piqui Chaqui, who meet in a street in Cuzco. Piqui Chaqui wants to get news, but to tell nothing, and in this he succeeds. The death of Inca Pachacuti is announced to him, and the accession of Tupac Yupanqui, and with this news he departs.

Next there is an interview between the new Inca Tupac Yupanqui, the Uillac Uma, and the defeated general Rumi–naui, who promises to retrieve the former disaster and bring the rebels to Cuzco, dead or alive. It after wards appears that the scheme of Rumi–naui was one of treachery. He intended to conceal his troops in eaves and gorges near Ollantay– tampu ready to rush in, when a signal was made. Rumi-naui then cut and slashed his face, covered himself with mud, and appeared at the gates of Ollantay–tampu, declaring that he had received this treatment from the new Inca, and imploring protection.[FN#5] Ollantay received him with the greatest kindness and hospitality. In a few days Ollantay and his people celebrated the Raymi or great festival of the sun with much rejoicing and drinking. Rumi-naui pretended to join in the festivities, but when most of them were wrapped in drunken sleep, he opened the gates, let in his own men, and made them all prisoners.

[FN#5] A bust, on an earthen vase, was presented to Don Antonio Maria Alvarez, the political chief of Cuzco, in 1837, by an Indian who declared that it had been handed down in his family from time immemorial, as a likeness of the general, Rumi–naui, who plays an important part in this drama of Ollantay. The person represented must have been a general, from the ornament on the forehead, called mascapaycha, and there are wounds cut on the face.—Museo Erudito, No. B.

There is next another scene in the garden of the convent, in which Yma Sumac importunes Pitu Salla to tell her the secret of the prisoner. Pitu Salla at last yields and opens a stone door. Cusi Coyllur is discovered, fastened to a wall, and in a dying state. She had been imprisoned, by order of her father, Inca Pachacuti on the birth of Yma Sumac. She is restored with food and water, and the relationship is discovered when Cusi Coyllur hears the child's name, for she had given it to her.

Next the Inca Tupac Yupanqui is discovered in the great hall of his palace, seated on his tiana or throne, with the Uillac Uma in attendance. To them enters a chasqui, or messenger, who describes the result of Rumi−naui's treachery in octosyllabic quatrains. Rumi−naui himself enters and receives the thanks of his sovereign. Then the prisoners are brought in guarded−Ollantay, Hanco Huayllu, Urco Huaranca, and Piqui Chaqui. The Inca upbraids them for their treason. He then asks the Uillac Uma for his judgment. The High Priest recommends mercy. Rumi−naui advises immediate execution: The Inca seems to concur and they are ordered off, when suddenly the Inca cries 'Stop.' He causes them all to be released, appoints Ollantay to the highest post in the empire next to himself, and Urco Huaranca to a high command. There are rejoicings, and in the midst of it all Yma Sumac forces her way into the hall, and throws herself at the Inca's feet, entreating him to save her mother from death. The Inca hands over the matter to Ollantay, but this Yma Sumac will not have, and, the Uillac Uma intervening, the Inca consents to go with the child.

The final scene is in the gardens of the convent. The Inca enters with Yma Sumac, followed by the whole strength of the company. Mama Ccacca is ordered to open the stone door and Cusi Coyllur is brought out. She proves to be the sister of the Inca and the wife of Ollantay. There are explanations, and all ends happily.

Of the antiquity of the drama of Ollantay there is now no question. General Mitre wrote an elaborate paper on its authenticity, raising several points to prove that it was of modern origin. But every point he raised has been satisfactorily refuted. At the same time there are many other points, some of them referred to by Zegarra, which establish the antiquity of the drama beyond any doubt. The antiquity of the name Ollantay−tampu, applied to the fortress in memory of the drama, is proved by its use in the narratives of Molina (1560) and of Salcamayhua.

An able review of the literature connected with the drama of Ollantay was written by Don E. Larrabure y Unanue, the present Vice−President of Peru, who considers that Ollantay would make a good acting play with magnificent scenic effects.

MS. TEXTS.

1. The original text of Valdez. In 1853 the property of Don Narciso Cuentas of Tinta, heir of Dr. Valdez.

Apu Ollantay

2. The Justiniani text. In 1853 at Laris. Copy of the Valdez text.

3. Markham's copy of the Justiniani text (printed 1871).

4. Rosas copy of the Justiniani text.

5. Copy in the convent of San Domingo at Cuzco (the Dominican text).

6. Von Tschudi's copy of the Dominican text (printed 1853).

7. Text of Zegarra (printed 1878).

8. Second text of von Tschudi.

9. Text of Spilsbury.

10. Text of Sahuaraura penes Dr. Gonzalez de la Rosa.

There is light thrown upon the name Ollantay by the evidence taken during the journey of the Viceroy Toledo from Jauja to Cuzco, from November 1570 to March 1571. He wanted information respecting the origin of the Inca government, and 200 witnesses were examined, the parentage or lineage of each witness being recorded. Among these we find six witnesses of the Antasayac ayllu. Sayac means a station or division, Anta is a small town near Cuzco. The names of the six Anta witnesses were

ANCAILLO; USCA; HUACRO;
MANCOY; AUCA PURI; ULLANTAY;

Besides ANTONIO PACROTRICA and PUNICU PAUCAR, Chiefs of Anta.

We thus find that the name of Ollantay belonged to Anta. Now the Incas were under great obligations to the chief of Anta, for that chief had rescued the eldest son of Inca Rocca from the chief of Ayamarca, and had restored him to his father. For this great service the chief of Anta was declared to be a noble of the highest rank and cousin to the Inca family. Moreover, the daughter of the Anta chief was married to the Inca Uira–cocha, and was the mother of Pachacuti. Assuming, as seems probable, that Ollantay was a son of the chief of Anta, he would be a cousin of the Inca, and of very high rank, though not an agnate of the reigning family. This, I take it, is what is intended. Pachacuti desired to raise his family high above all others, and that, consequently, there should be no marriages with subjects even of the highest rank; and his excessive severity on the transgression of his rule by his daughter is thus explained.

OLLANTAY

ACTS AND SCENES

ACT 1.

Sc. 1.—Open space near Cuzco. Ollantay, Piqui Chaqui, Uillac Uma.

Sc. 2.—Hall in the Colcampata. Anahuarqui, Cusi Coyllur, Inca Pachacuti, Boys and Girls, Singers.

Sc. 3.—Hall in the Inca's palace. Pachacuti, Rumi–naui, Ollantay.

Sc. 4.—Height above Cuzco. Ollantay, Piqui Chaqui, Unseen Singer.

Sc. 5.—Hall in the Inca's palace. Pachacuti, Rumi–naui, and a Chasqui.

ACT II.

Sc. 1.—Ollantay–tampu Hall. Ollantay, Urco Huaranca, Hanco Huayllu, People and Soldiers.

Sc. 2.—A wild place in the mountains. Rumi–naui's soliloquy.

Sc. 3.—Gardens of the Virgins. Yma Sumac, Pitu Salla, Mama Ccacca.

ACT III.

Sc. 1.—Pampa Maroni at Cuzco. Uillac Uma and Piqui Chaqui.

Sc. 2.—Palace of Tupac Yupanqui. Tupac Yupanqui, Uillac Uma, Rumi–naui.

Sc. 3.—Ollantay–tampu, Terrace. Rumi–naui, Ollantay, Guards.

Sc. 4.—House of Virgins, Corridor. Yma Sumac, Pitu Salla.

Sc. 5.—House of Virgins, Garden. Yma Sumac, Pitu Salla, Cusi Coyllur.

Sc. 6.—Palace of Tupac Yupanqui. Tupac Yupanqui, Uillac Uma, a Chasqui, Rumi–naui, Ollantay, Urco Huaranca, Hanco Huayllu, Piqui Chaqui, Chiefs and Guards. then Yma Sumac.

Sc. 7.—House of Virgins, Garden. All of Scene 6, and Mama Ccacca, Cusi Coyllur, Pitu Salla.

OLLANTAY DRAMATIS PERSONAE

SCENE

In Cuzco and its environs, and Ollantay–tampu

DRAMATIS PERSONAE

APU OLLANTAY.—General of Anti–suyu, the eastern province of the empire. A young chief, but not of the blood–royal. His rank was that of a Tucuyricuo or Viceroy. The name occurs among the witnesses examined by order of the Viceroy Toledo, being one of the six of the Antasayac ayllu.

PACHACUTI.—The Sovereign Inca.

TUPAC YUPANQUI.—Sovereign. Inca, son and heir of Pachacuti.

RUMI–NAUI.—A great chief, General of Colla–suyu. The word means 'Stone–eye.'

UILLAC UMA.—High Priest of the Sun. The word Uma means head, and Uillac, a

12

councillor and diviner.

URCO HUARANCA.—A chief. The words mean' Mountain Chief.' The word huaranca means 1000; hence, Chief of a Thousand.

HANCO HUAYLLU AUQUI.—An old officer, of the blood–royal.

PIQUI CHAQUI.—Page to Ollantay. The words mean 'fleet–footed.'

ANAHUARQUI.—The Ccoya or Queen, wife of Pachacuti.

CUSI COYLLUR NUSTA.—A Princess, daughter of Pachacuti. The words mean 'the joyful star.'

YMA SUMAC.—Daughter of Cusi Coyllur. The words mean 'How beautiful.'

PITU SALLA.—A girl, companion of Yma Sumac.

CCACCA MAMA.—A matron of Virgins of the Sun. Jailer of Cusi Coyllur.

Nobles, captains, soldiers, boys and girls dancing, singers, attendants, messengers or Chasqui.

ACT I

SCENE I

An open space near the junction of the two torrents of Cuzco, the Huatanay and Tullumayu or Rodadero, called Pumap Chupan, just outside the gardens of the Sun. The Temple of the Sun beyond the gardens, and the Sacsahuaman hill surmounted by the fortress, rising in the distance. The palace of Colcampata on the hillside.

(Enter OLLANTAY L. [in a gilded tunic, breeches of llama sinews, usutas or shoes of llama hide, a red mantle of ccompi or fine cloth, and the chucu or head–dress of his rank, holding a battle–axe (champi) and club (macana)] and PIQUI CHAQUI coming up from the back R. [in a coarse brown tunic of auasca or llama cloth, girdle used as a sling, and chucu or head–dress of a Cuzqueno].)

Ollantay.

Where, young fleet–foot, hast thou been?
Hast thou the starry nusta seen?

Apu Ollantay

Piqui Chaqui.

The Sun forbids such sacrilege
'Tis not for me to see the star.
Dost thou, my master, fear no ill,
Thine eyes upon the Inca's child?

Ollantay.

In spite of all I swear to love
That tender dove, that lovely star;
My heart is as a lamb[FN#6] with her,
And ever will her presence seek.

[FN#6] Chita is the lamb of the llama. A lamb of two or three months was a favourite pet in the time of the Incas. It followed its mistress, adorned with a little bell and ribbons.

Piqui Chaqui.

Such thoughts are prompted by Supay[FN#7];
That evil being possesses thee.
All round are beauteous girls to choose
Before old age, and weakness come.
If the great Inca knew thy plot
And what thou seekest to attain,
Thy head would fall by his command,
Thy body would be quickly burnt.

[FN#7] Supay, an evil spirit, according to some authorities.

15

Apu Ollantay

Ollantay.

Boy, do not dare to cross me thus.
One more such word and thou shalt die.
These hands will tear thee limb from limb,
If still thy councils are so base.

Piqui Chaqui.

Well! treat thy servant as a dog,
But do not night and day repeat,
'Piqui Chaqui! swift of foot!
Go once more to seek the star.'

Ollantay.

Have I not already said
That e'en if death's fell scythe[FN#8] was here,
If mountains should oppose my path
Like two fierce foes[FN#9] who block the way,
Yet will I fight all these combined
And risk all else to gain my end,
And whether it be life or death
I'll cast myself at Coyllur's feet.

[FN#8] Ichuna, a sickle or scythe. The expression has been cited by
General Mitre and others as an argument that the drama is modern,
because this is a metaphor confined to the old world. But ichuna was in
use, in Quichua, in this sense, before the Spaniards came. The word is
from Ichu, grass.

[FN#9] The Peruvians personified a mountain as two spirits, good and evil. In writing poetically of a mountain opposing, it would be referred to in the persons of its genii or spirits, and spoken of as two foes, not one.

Piqui Chaqui.

Rut if Supay himself should come?

Ollantay.

I'd strike the evil spirit down.

Piqui Chaqui.

If thou shouldst only see his nose,
Thou wouldst not speak as thou dost now.

Ollantay.

Now, Piqui Chaqui, speak the truth,
Seek not evasion or deceit.
Dost thou not already know,
Of all the flowers in the field,
Not one can equal my Princess?

Apu Ollantay

Piqui Chaqui.

Still, my master, thou dost rave.
I think I never saw thy love.
Stay! was it her who yesterday
Came forth with slow and faltering steps
And sought a solitary[FN#10] path[FN#11]?
If so, 'tis true she's like the sun,
The moon less beauteous than her face.[FN#12]

[FN#10] Rurun, desert, solitude.

[FN#11] Tasquiy, to march; tasquina, promenade, path.

[FN#12] Cusi Coyllur, while daylight lasted, was, in the eyes of Piqui Chaqui, like the sun. A change takes place at twilight, and at night she is like the moon.

Ollantay.

It surely was my dearest love.
How beautiful, how bright is she
This very moment thou must go
And take my message to the Star.

Piqui Chaqui.

I dare not, master; in the day,
I fear to pass the palace gate.
With all the splendour of the court,
I could not tell her from the rest.

Ollantay.

Didst thou not say thou sawest her?

Piqui Chaqui.

I said so, but it was not sense.
A star can only shine at night
Only at night could I be sure.

Ollantay.

Begone, thou lazy good–for–nought.
The joyful star that I adore,
If placed in presence of the Sun,
Would shine as brightly as before.

Piqui Chaqui.

Lo! some person hither comes,
Perhaps an old crone seeking alms;
Yes! Look! he quite resembles one.

Lot him the dangerous message take.
Send it by him, O noble Chief!
From me they would not hear the tale;
Thy page is but a humble lad.

(Enter the UILLAC UMA, or High Priest of the Sun, at the back, arms
raised to the Sun. In a grey tunic and black mantle from the shoulders
to the ground, a long knife in his belt, the undress chucu on his head.)

Uillac Uma.

O giver of all warmth and light
O Sun! I fall and worship thee.
For thee the victims are prepared,
A thousand llamas and their lambs
Are ready for thy festal day.
The sacred fire'll lap their blood,
In thy dread presence, mighty one,
After long fast[FN#13] thy victims fall.

[FN#13] Fasting was a preparation for all great religious ceremonies.
Victims for sacrifice underwent a previous fast, which was looked upon
in the fight of purification before being offered to the Deity.

Ollantay.

Who comes hither, Piqui Chaqui?
Yes, 'tis the holy Uillac Uma;
He brings his tools of augury.
No puma[FN#14] more astute and wise
I hate that ancient conjurer
Who prophesies of evil things,

I feel the evils he foretells;
'Tis he who ever brings ill-luck.

[FN#14] They gave the attributes we usually assign to the fox to the
puma.

Piqui Chaqui.

Silence, master, do not speak,
The old man doubly is informed;
Fore-knowing every word you say,
Already he has guessed it all.

(He lies down on a bank.)

Ollantay (aside).

He sees me. I must speak to him.

(The Uillac Uma comes forward.)

O Uillac Uma, Great High Priest,
I bow before thee with respect
May the skies be clear for thee,
And brightest sunshine meet thine eyes.

Uillac Uma.

Brave Ollantay! Princely one!
May all the teeming land be thine;

Apu Ollantay

May thy far–reaching arm of might
Reduce the wide–spread universe.

Ollantay.

Old man! thine aspect causes fear,
Thy presence here some ill forebodes;
All round thee dead men's bones appear,
Baskets, flowers, sacrifice.
All men when they see thy face
Are filled with terror and alarm.
What means it all? why comest thou?
It wants some months before the least.
Is it that the Inca is ill?
Perchance hast thou some thought divined
Which soon will turn to flowing blood.
Why comest thou? the Sun's great day,
The Moon's libations are not yet
The moon has not yet nearly reached
The solemn time for sacrifice.
Uillac Uma. Why dost thou these questions put,
In tones of anger and reproach?
Am I, forsooth, thy humble slave?
That I know all I'll quickly prove.

Ollantay.

My beating heart is filled with dread,
Beholding thee so suddenly;
Perchance thy coming is a sign,
Of evils overtaking me.

Apu Ollantay

Uillac Uma.

Fear not, Ollantay! not for that,
The High Priest comes to thee this day.
It is perhaps for love of thee,
That, as a straw is blown by wind,
A friend, this day, encounters thee.
Speak to me as to a friend,
Hide nothing from my scrutiny.
This day I come to offer thee
A last and most momentous choice
'Tis nothing less than life or death.

Ollantay.

Then make thy words more clear to me,
That I may understand the choice
Till now 'tis but a tangled skein,
Unravel it that I may know.

Uillac Uma.

'Tis well. Now listen, warlike. Chief
My science has enabled me,
To learn and see all hidden things
Unknown to other mortal men.
My power will enable me
To make of thee a greater prince.
I brought thee up from tender years,
And cherished thee with love and care

Apu Ollantay

I now would guide thee in the right,
And ward off all that threatens thee.
As chief of Anti–suyu now,
The people venerate thy name;
Thy Sovereign trusts and honours thee,
E'en to sharing half his realm.
From all the rest he chose thee out,
And placed all power in thy hands;
He made thy armies great and strong,
And strengthened thee against thy foes
How numerous soe'er they be,
They have been hunted down by thee.
Are these good reasons for thy wish,
To wound thy Sovereign to the heart?
His daughter is beloved by thee;
Thy passion thou wouldst fain indulge,
Lawless and forbidden though it be.
I call upon thee, stop in time,
Tear this folly from thy heart.
If thy passion is immense,
Still let honour hold its place.
You reel, you stagger on the brink
I'd snatch thee from the very edge.
Thou knowest well it cannot be,
The Inca never would consent.
If thou didst e'en propose it now,
He would be overcome with rage;
From favoured prince and trusted chief,
Thou wouldst descend to lowest rank.

Ollantay.

How is it that thou canst surely know
What still is hidden in my heart?

24

Apu Ollantay

Her mother only knows my love,
Yet thou revealest all to me.

Uillac Uma.

I read thy secret on the moon,
As if upon the Quipu knots;
And what thou wouldst most surely hide,
Is plain to me as all the rest.

Ollantay.

In my heart I had divined
That thou wouldst search me through and through
Thou knowest all, O Councillor,
And wilt thou now desert thy son?

Uillac Uma.

How oft we mortals heedless drink,
A certain death from golden cup
Recall to mind how ills befall,
And that a stubborn heart 's the cause.
Ollantay (kneeling).

Plunge that dagger in my breast,
Thou holdst it ready in thy belt;
Cut out my sad and broken heart

Apu Ollantay

I ask the favour at thy feet.

Uillac Uma (to Piqui Chaqui).

Gather me that flower, boy.

(Piqui Chaqui gives him a withered flower and lies down again, pretending to sleep.)

(To Ollantay).

Behold, it is quite dead and dry.
Once more behold! e'en now it weeps,
It weeps. The water flows from it.

(Water flows out of the flower.)

Ollantay.

More easy for the barren rocks
Or for sand to send forth water,
Than that I should cease to love
The fair princess, the joyful star.

Uillac Uma.

Put a seed into the ground,
It multiplies a hundredfold;

The more thy crime shall grow and swell,
The greater far thy sudden fall.

Ollantay.

Once for all, I now confess
To thee, O great and mighty Priest;
Now learn my fault. To thee I speak,
Since thou hast torn it from my heart.
The lasso to tie me is long,
'Tis ready to twist round my throat
Yet its threads are woven with gold,
It avenges a brilliant crime.
Cusi Coyllur e'en now is my wife,
Already we 're bound and are one;
My blood now runs in her veins,
E'en now I am noble as she.
Her mother has knowledge of all,
The Queen can attest what I say;
Let me tell all this to the King,
I pray for thy help and advice.
I will speak without fear and with force,
He may perhaps give way to his rage
Yet he may consider my youth,
May remember the battles I've fought;
The record is carved on my club.

(Holds up his macana.)

He may think of his enemies crushed,
The thousands I've thrown at his feet.

Uillac Uma.

Apu Ollantay

Young Prince! thy words are too bold,
Thou hast twisted the thread of thy fate—
Beware, before 'tis too late;
Disentangle and weave it afresh,
Go alone to speak to the King,
Alone bear the blow that you seek;
Above all let thy words be but few,
And say them with deepest respect;
Be it life, be it death that you find,
I will never forget thee, my son.

(Walks up and exit.)

Ollantay.

Ollantay, thou art a man,
No place in thy heart for fear;
Cusi Coyllur, surround me with light.
Piqui Chaqui, where art thou?

Piqui Chaqui (jumping up).

I was asleep, my master,
And dreaming of evil things.

Ollantay.

Of what?

Piqui Chaqui.

Of a fox with a rope round its neck.

Ollantay.

Sure enough, thou art the fox.

Piqui Chaqui.

It is true that my nose is growing finer,
And my ears a good deal longer.

Ollantay.

Come, lead me to the Coyllur.

Piqui Chaqui.

It is still daylight.

(Exeunt.)

SCENE 2

A great hall in the Colcampata, then the palace of the Queen or Ccoya Anahuarqui. In the centre of the back scene a doorway, and seen through it gardens with the snowy peak of Vilcanota in the distance. Walls covered with golden slabs. On either side of the doorway three recesses, with household gods in the shape of maize–cobs and llamas, and gold vases in them. On R. a golden tiana or throne. On L. two lower seats covered with cushions of fine woollen cloth.

(ANAHUARQUI, the Queen or Ccoya (in blue chucu, white cotton bodice, and red mantle secured by a golden topu or pin, set with emeralds, and a blue skirt), and the princess CUSI COYLLUR (in a chucu, with feathers of the tunqui, white bodice and skirt, and grey mantle with topu, set with pearls) discovered seated.)

Anahuarqui.

Since when art thou feeling so sad,
Cusi Coyllur! great Inti's prunelle?[FN#15]
Since when hast thou lost all thy joy,
Thy smile and thy once merry laugh?

[FN#15] Intip llirpun, 'apple of the sun's eye.' There is no English equivalent that is suitable.

Tears of grief now pour down my face,
As I watch and mourn over my child;
Thy grief makes me ready to die.
Thy union filled thee with joy,
Already you're really his wife.
Is he not the man of thy choice?
O daughter, devotedly loved,

Apu Ollantay

Why plunged in such terrible grief?

(Cusi Coyllur has had her face hidden in the pillows. She now rises to her feet, throwing up her arms.)

Cusi Coyllur.

O my mother! O most gracious Queen!
How can my tears o'er cease to flow,
How can my bitter sighs surcease,
While the valiant Chief I worship
For many days and sleepless nights,
All heedless of my tender years,
Seems quite to have forgotten me?
He has turned his regard from his wife
And no longer seeks for his love.
O my mother! O most gracious Queen!
O my husband so beloved!
Since the day when I last saw my love
The moon has been hidden from view;
The sun shines no more as of old,
In rising it rolls among mist;
At night the stars are all dim,
All nature seems sad and distressed
The comet with fiery tail,
Announces my sorrow and grief
Surrounded by darkness and tears,
Evil auguries fill me with fears.
O my mother! O most gracious Queen!
O my husband so beloved!

Anahuarqui.

Apu Ollantay

Compose thyself and dry thine eyes,
The King, thy father, has arrived.
Thou lovest Ollantay, my child?

(Enter the INCA PACHACUTI. On his head the mascapaycha, with the llautu
or imperial fringe. A tunic of cotton embroidered with gold; on his
breast the golden breastplate representing the sun, surrounded by the
calendar of months. Round his waist the fourfold belt of tocapu. A
crimson mantle of fine vicuna wool, fastened on his shoulders by golden
puma's heads. Shoes of cloth of gold. He sits down on the golden tiana.)

Inca Pachacuti.

Cusi Coyllur! Star of joy,
Most lovely of my progeny!
Thou symbol of parental love—
Thy lips are like the huayruru.[FN#16]
Rest upon thy father's breast,
Repose, my child, within mine arms.

[FN#16] Huayruru is the seed of a thorny bush, erythrina rubra, of a
bright red colour. Zegarra has coral as the equivalent for huayruru.

(Cusi Coyllur comes across. They embrace.)

Unwind thyself, my precious one,
A thread of gold within the woof.
All my happiness rests upon thee,
Thou art my greatest delight.
Thine eyes are lovely and bright,
As the rays of my father the Sun.
When thy lips are moving to speak,
When thine eyelids are raised with a smile,

32

Apu Ollantay

The wide world is fairly entranced.
Thy breathing embalms the fresh air;
Without thee thy father would pine,
Life to him would be dreary and waste.
He seeks for thy happiness, child,
Thy welfare is ever his care.

(Cusi Coyllur throws herself at his feet.)

Cusi Coyllur.

O father, thy kindness to me
I feel; and embracing thy knees
All the grief of thy daughter will cease,
At peace when protected by thee.
Pachacuti. How is this! my daughter before me
On knees at my feet, and in tears?
I fear some evil is near—
Such emotion must needs be explained.

Cusi Coyllur.

The star does weep before Inti,
The limpid tears wash grief away.
Pachacuti. Rise, my beloved, my star,
Thy place is on thy dear father's knee.

(Cusi Coyllur rises and sits on a stool by her father. An attendant
approaches.)

Attendant.

Apu Ollantay

O King! thy servants come to please thee.

Pachacuti.

Let them all enter.

(Boys and girls enter dancing. After the dance they sing a harvest song.)

Thou must not feed,
O Tuyallay,[FN#17]
In nusta's field,
O Tuyallay.
Thou must not rob,
O Tuyallay,
The harvest maize,
O Tuyallay.

[FN#17] The tuya (coccoborus chrysogaster) is a small finch, and
tuyallay means 'my little tuya.'

The grains are white,
O Tuyallay,
So sweet for food,
O Tuyallay.
The fruit is sweet,
O Tuyallay,
The leaves are green
O Tuyallay;
But the trap is set,
O Tuyallay.
The lime is there,
O Tuyallay.
We'll cut thy claws,

O Tuyallay,
To seize thee quick,
O Tuyallay.
Ask Piscaca,[FN#18]
O Tuyallay,
Nailed on a branch,
O Tuyallay.
Where is her heart,
O Tuyallay?
Where her plumes,
O Tuyallay?
She is cut up,
O Tuyallay,
For stealing grain,
O Tuyallay.
See the fate,
O Tuyallay,
Of robber birds,
O Tuyallay.

[FN#18] The piscaca is a much larger bird than the tuya. These piscacas
(coccoborus torridus) are nailed to trees as a warning to other birds.
They are black, with white breasts.

Pachacuti.

Cusi Coyllur, remain thou here,
Thy mother's palace is thy home
Fail not to amuse thyself,
Surrounded by thy maiden friends.

(Exeunt the Inca Pachacuti, the Ccoya Anahuarqui, and attendants.)

Apu Ollantay

Cusi Coyllur.

I should better like a sadder song.
My dearest friends, the last you sang
To me foreshadowed evil things;[FN#19]
You who sang it leave me now.

[FN#19] In the tuya she sees her husband Ollantay, while the poor
princess herself is the forbidden grain.

(Exeunt boys and girls, except one girl who sings.)

Two loving birds are in despair,[FN#20]
They moan, they weep, they sigh;
For snow has fallen on the pair,
To hollow tree they fly.

[FN#20] This is a yarahui or mournful elegy, of which there are so many
in the Quichua language. The singers of them were known as yarahuec.

But lo! one dove is left alone
And mourns her cruel fate;
She makes a sad and piteous moan,
Alone without a mate.
She fears her friend is dead and gone—
Confirmed in her belief,
Her sorrow finds relief in song,
And thus she tells her grief.
'Sweet mate! Alas, where art thou now?
I miss thine eyes so bright,
Thy feet upon the tender bough,
Thy breast so pure and bright.'
She wanders forth from stone to stone,
She seeks her mate in vain;

36

'My love! my love!' she makes her moan,
She falls, she dies in pain.
Cusi Coyllur. That yarahui is too sad,
Leave me alone.

(Exit the girl who sang the yarahui.)

Now my tears can freely flow.

SCENE 3

Great hall in the palace of Pachacuti. The INCA, as before, discovered
seated on a golden tiana L. Enter to him R. OLLANTAY and RUMI–NAUI.

Pachacuti.

The time has arrived, O great Chiefs,
To decide on the coming campaign.
The spring is approaching us now,
And our army must start for the war.
To the province of Colla[FN#21] we march—
There is news of Chayanta's[FN#22] advance.
The enemies muster in strength,
They sharpen their arrows and spears.

[FN#21] Colla–suyu, the basin of lake Titicaca.

[FN#22] Chayanta, a tribe in the montana south of the Collas.

Ollantay. O King, that wild rabble untaught
Can never resist thine array;

Apu Ollantay

Cuzco alone with its height
Is a barrier that cannot be stormed.
Twenty four thousand of mine,
With their champis[FN#23] selected with care,
Impatiently wait for the sign,
The sound of the beat of my drums,[FN#24]
The strains of my clarion and fife.

[FN#23] Champi, a one–handed battle–axe.

[FN#24] Huancar, a drum; pututu, fife.

Pachacuti.

Strive then to stir them to fight,
Arouse them to join in the fray,
Lest some should desire to yield,
To escape the effusion of blood.

Rumi–naui.

The enemies gather in force,
The Yuncas[FN#25] are called to their aid;
They have put on their garbs for the war,
And have stopped up the principal roads.
All this is to hide their defects—
The men of Chayanta are base.
We hear they're destroying the roads,
But we can force open the way;
Our llamas are laden with food—
We are ready to traverse the wilds.

[FN#25] Yunca, inhabitant of warm valley. Here it refers to the wild tribes of the montana.

Pachacuti.

Are you really ready to start
To punish those angry snakes?
But first you must give them a chance
To surrender, retiring in peace,
So that blood may not flow without cause,
That no deaths of my soldiers befall.

Ollantay.

I am ready to march with my men,
Every detail prepared and in place,
But alas! I am heavy with care,
Almost mad with anxious suspense.

Pachacuti.

Speak, Ollantay. Tell thy wish—
'Tis granted, e'en my royal fringe.

Ollantay.

Hear me in secret, O King.

Apu Ollantay

Pachacuti (to Rumi−naui).

Noble Chief of Colla, retire;
Seek repose in thy house for a time.
I will call thee before very long,
Having need of thy valour and skill.

Rumi−naui.

With respect I obey thy command.

(Exit Rumi−naui.)

Ollantay.

Thou knowest, O most gracious Lord,
That I have served thee from a youth,
Have worked with fortitude and truth,
Thy treasured praise was my reward.[FN#26]
All dangers I have gladly met,
For thee I always watched by night,
For thee was forward in the fight,
My forehead ever bathed in sweat.
For thee I've been a savage foe,
Urging my Antis[FN#27] not to spare,
But kill and fill the land with fear,
And make the blood of conquered flow.
My name is as a dreaded rope,[FN#28]
I've made the hardy Yuncas[FN#29] yield,
By me the fate of Chancas[FN#30] sealed,

40

They are thy thralls without a hope.

[FN#26] In the original Quichua, Ollantay makes his appeal to the Inca in quatrains of octosyllabic verses, the first line rhyming with the last, and the second with the third. Garcilasso de la Vega and others testify to the proficiency of the Incas in this form of composition.

[FN#27] Ollantay was Viceroy of Anti–suyu.

[FN#28] Chahuar, a rope of aloe fibre. A curb or restraint.

[FN#29] Raprancutan cuchurcani: literally, 'I have clipped their wings.' Rapra, a wing.

[FN#30] The powerful nation of Chancas, with their chief, Huancavilca, inhabited the great valley of Andahuaylas and were formidable rivals of the Incas. But they were subdued by Pachacuti long before Ollantay can have been born. An allowable dramatic anachronism.

'Twas I who struck the fatal blow,
When warlike Huancavilca[FN#31] rose,
Disturbing thy august repose,
And laid the mighty traitor low.

[FN#31] Huancavilca was chief of the powerful nation of Chancas.

Ollantay ever led the van,
Wherever men were doomed to die;
When stubborn foes were forced to fly,
Ollantay ever was the man.

Now every tribe bows down to thee—
Some nations peacefully were led,

Those that resist their blood is shed—
But all, O King, was due to me.
O Sovereign Inca, great and brave,
Rewards I know were also mine,
My gratitude and thanks are thine,
To me the golden axe you gave.
Inca! thou gavest me command
And rule o'er all the Anti race,
To me they ever yield with grace,
And thine, great King, is all their land
My deeds, my merits are thine own
To thee alone my work is due.
For one more favour I would sue,
My faithful service—thy renown.

(Ollantay kneels before the Inca.)

Thy thrall: I bow to thy behest,
Thy fiat now will seal my fate.
O King, my services are great,
I pray thee grant one last request.
I ask for Cusi Coyllur's hand
If the Nusta's[FN#32] love I've won.
O King! you'll have a faithful son,
Fearless, well tried, at thy command.

[FN#32] Nusta, Princess.

Pachacuti.

Ollantay, thou dost now presume.
Thou art a subject, nothing more.
Remember, bold one, who thou art,
And learn to keep thy proper place.

Ollantay.

Strike me to the heart.

Pachacuti.

'Tis for me to see to that,
And not for thee to choose.
Thy presumption is absurd.
Be gone!

(Ollantay rises and exit R.)

SCENE 4

A rocky height above Cuzco to the NE. Distant view of the city of Cuzco
and of the Sacsahuaman hill, crowned by the fortress.

(Enter OLLANTAY armed.)

Ollantay.

Alas, Ollantay! Ollantay!
Thou master of so many lands,
Insulted by him thou servedst well.
O my thrice–beloved Coyllur,
Thee too I shall lose for ever.
O the void[FN#33] within my heart,
O my princess! O precious dove!

Apu Ollantay

Cuzco! O thou beautiful city!
Henceforth behold thine enemy.

[FN#33] Pisipachiyqui, to suffer from the void caused by absence.
Pisipay, to regret the absence of, to miss any one.

I'll bare thy breast to stab thy heart,
And throw it as food for condors;
Thy cruel Inca I will slay.
I will call my men in thousands,
The Antis will be assembled,
Collected as with a lasso.
All will be trained, all fully armed,
I will guide them to Sacsahuaman.
They will be as a cloud of curses,
When flames rise to the heavens.
Cuzco shall sleep on a bloody couch,
The King shall perish in its fall;
Then shall my insulter see
How numerous are my followers.
When thou, proud King, art at my feet,
We then shall see if thou wilt say,
'Thou art too base for Coyllur's hand.'
Not then will I bow down and ask,
For I, not thou, will be the King—
Yet, until then, let prudence rule.

(Enter PIQUI CHAQUI from back, R.)

Piqui Chaqui, go back with speed,
Tell the Princess I come to–night.

Piqui Chaqui.

Apu Ollantay

I have only just come from there—
The palace was deserted quite,
No soul to tell me what had passed,
Not even a dog[FN#34] was there.

[FN#34] The Dominican text has misi, a cat, instead of allco, a dog.
Von Tschudi thought that misi was a word of Spanish origin. Zegarra says
that it is not. Before the Spaniards came, there was a small wild cat in
the Andes called misi–puna. But the Justiniani text has allco, a dog.

All the doors were closed and fastened,
Except the principal doorway,
And that was left without a guard.

Ollantay.

And the servants?

Piqui Chaqui.

Even the mice had fled and gone,
For nothing had been left to eat.
Only an owl was brooding there,
Uttering its cry of evil omen.

Ollantay.

Perhaps then her father has taken her,
To hide her in his palace bounds.

45

Apu Ollantay

Piqui Chaqui.

The Inca may have strangled her;
Her mother too has disappeared.

Ollantay.

Did no one ask for me
Before you went away?

Piqui Chaqui.

Near a thousand men are seeking
For you, and all are enemies,
Armed with their miserable clubs.

Ollantay.

If they all arose against me,
With this arm I'd fight them all
No one yet has beat this hand,
Wielding the champi sharp and true.

Piqui Chaqui.

I too would like to give a stroke

At least, if my enemy was unarmed.

Ollantay.

To whom?

Piqui Chaqui.

I mean that Urco Huaranca chief,
Who lately was in search of thee.

Ollantay.

Perhaps the Inca sends him here
If so my anger is aroused.

Piqui Chaqui.

Not from the King, I am assured,
He cometh of his own accord
And yet he is an ignoble man.

Ollantay.

He has left Cuzco, I believe;
My own heart tells me it is so

I'm sure that owl announces it.
We'll take to the hills, at once.

Piqui Chaqui.

But wilt thou abandon the Star?

Ollantay.

What can I do, alas!
Since she has disappeared?
Alas, my dove! my sweet princess.

(Music heard among the rocks.)

Piqui Chaqui.

Listen to that yarahui,
The sound comes from somewhere near.

(They sit on rocks.)

SONG

**In a moment I lost my beloved,
She was gone, and I never knew where;
I sought her in fields and in woods,
Asking all if they 'd seen the Coyllur.**
Her face was so lovely and fair,
They called her the beautiful Star.

Apu Ollantay

No one else can be taken for her,
With her beauty no girl can compare.
Both the sun and the moon seem to shine,
Resplendent they shine from a height,
Their rays to her beauty resign
Their brilliant light with delight.
Her hair is a soft raven black,
Her tresses are bound with gold thread,
They fall in long folds down her back,
And add charm to her beautiful head.
Her eyelashes brighten her face,
Two rainbows less brilliant and fair,
Her eyes full of mercy and grace,
With nought but two, suns can compare.
The eyelids with arrows concealed,
Gaily shoot their rays into the heart
They open, lo! beauty revealed,
Pierces through like a glittering dart.
Her cheeks Achancara[FN#35] on snow,
Her face more fair than the dawn,
From her mouth the laughter doth flow,
Between pearls as bright as the morn.

[FN#35] Achancara, a begonia. A red flower in the neighbourhood of
Cuzco, according to Zegarra. One variety is red and white.

Smooth as crystal and spotlessly clear
Is her throat, like the corn in a sheaf
Her bosoms, which scarcely appear,
Like flowers concealed by a leaf.
Her beautiful hand is a sight,
As it rests from all dangers secure,
Her fingers transparently white,
Like icicles spotless and pure.

Apu Ollantay

Ollantay (rising).

That singer, unseen and unknown,
Has declared Coyllur's beauty and grace;
He should fly hence, where grief overwhelms.
O Princess! O loveliest Star,
I alone am the cause of thy death,
I also should die with my love.

Piqui Chaqui.

Perhaps thy star has passed away,
For the heavens are sombre and grey.

Ollantay.

When they know that their Chief has fled,
My people will rise at my call,
They will leave the tyrant in crowds
And he will be nearly alone.

Piqui Chaqui.

Thou hast love and affection from men,
For thy kindness endears thee to all,
For thy hand's always open with gifts,
And is closely shut only to me.

Apu Ollantay

Ollantay.

Of what hast thou need?

Piqui Chaqui.

What? the means to got this and that,
To offer a gift to my girl,
To let others see what I have,
So that I may be held in esteem.

Ollantay.

Be as brave as thou art covetous,
And all the world will fear thee.

Piqui Chaqui.

My face is not suited for that;
Always gay and ready to laugh,
My features are not shaped that way.
To look brave! not becoming to me.
What clarions sound on the hills?
It quickly cometh near to us.

(Both look out at different sides.)

Ollantay.

I doubt not those who seek me—come,
Let us depart and quickly march.

Piqui Chaqui.

When flight is the word, I am here.

(Exeunt.)

SCENE 5

The great hall of the palace of Pachacuti. The INCA, as before, seated
on the tiana. Enter to him RUMI–NAUI.

Pachacuti.

I ordered a search to be made,
But Ollantay was not to be found.
My rage I can scarcely control—
Hast thou found this infamous wretch?

Rumi–naui.

His fear makes him hide from thy wrath.

Apu Ollantay

Pachacuti.

Take a thousand men fully armed,
And at once commence the pursuit.

Rumi−naui.

Who can tell what direction to take?
Three days have gone by since his flight,
Perchance he's concealed in some house,
And till now he is there, safely hid.

(Enter a chasqui or messenger with quipus.)

Behold, O King, a messenger
From Urubamba he has come.

Chasqui.

I was ordered to come to my King,
Swift as the wind, and behold me.

Pachacuti.

What news bringest thou?

Chasqui.

Apu Ollantay

This quipu will tell thee, O King.

Pachacuti.

Examine it, O Rumi−naui.

Rumi−naui.

Behold the llanta, and the knots[FN#36]
Announce the number of his men.

[FN#36] The llanta is the main rope of the quipu, about a yard long.
The small cords of llama wool, of various colours, denoting different
subjects, each with various kinds of knots, recording numbers.

Pachacuti (to Chasqui).

And thou, what hast thou seen?

Chasqui.

'Tis said that all the Anti host
Received Ollantay with acclaim;
Many have seen, and they recount,
Ollantay wears the royal fringe.

Rumi–naui.

The quipu record says the same.

Pachacuti.

Scarcely can I restrain my rage!
Brave chief, commence thy march at once,
Before the traitor gathers strength.
If thy force is not enough,
Add fifty thousand men of mine.
Advance at once with lightning speed,
And halt not till the foe is reached.

Rumi–naui.

To–morrow sees me on the route,
I go to call the troops at once
The rebels on the Colla road,
I drive them flying down the rocks.
Thine enemy I bring to thee,
Dead or alive, Ollantay falls.
Meanwhile, O Inca, mighty Lord,
Rest and rely upon thy thrall.

(Exeunt.)

END OF ACT I.

ACT II

SCENE 1

Ollantay–tampu. Hall of the fortress–palace. Back scene seven immense
stone, slabs, resting on them a monolith right across. Above masonry.
At sides masonry with recesses; in the R. centre a great doorway. A
golden tiana against the central slab.

(Enter OLLANTAY and URCO HUARANCA, both fully armed.)

Urco Huaranca.

Ollantay, thou hast been proclaimed
By all the Antis as their Lord.
The women weep, as you will see—
They lose their husbands and their sons,
Ordered to the Chayanta war.
When will there be a final stop
To distant wars? Year after year
They send us all to far–off lands,
Where blood is made to flow like rain.
The King himself is well supplied
With coca and all kinds of food.
What cares he that his people starve?
Crossing the wilds our llamas die,
Our feet are wounded by the thorns,
And if we would not die of thirst
We carry water on our backs.

Ollantay.

Gallant friends! Ye hear those words,
Ye listen to the mountain chief.
Filled with compassion for my men,
I thus, with sore and heavy heart,
Have spoken to the cruel king:
'The Anti–suyu must have rest;
All her best men shan't die for thee,
By battle, fire, and disease—
They die in numbers terrible.
How many men have ne'er returned,
How many chiefs have met their death
For enterprises far away?'
For this I left the Inca's court,[FN#37]
Saying that we must rest in peace;
Lot none of us forsake our hearths,
And if the Inca still persists,
Proclaim with him a mortal feud.

[FN#37] This, as we have seen, was not the reason why Ollantay fled from
Cuzco; but, from a leader's point of view, it was an excellent reason to
give to the people of Anti–suyu. The great wars of the Incas were, to
some extent, a heavy drain upon the people, but the recruiting was
managed with such skill, and was so equally divided among a number of
provinces, that it was not much felt.

(Enter HANCO HUAYLLU, several chiefs, and a great crowd of soldiers and
people.)

People.

Apu Ollantay

Long Eve our king, Ollantay
Bring forth the standard and the fringe,
Invest him with the crimson fringe
In Tampu now the Inca reigns,
He rises like the star of day.

(The chiefs, soldiers, and people range them selves round. Ollantay is
seated on the tiana by Hanco Huayllu, an aged Auqui or Prince.)

Hanco Huayllu.

Receive from me the royal fringe,
'Tis given by the people's will.
Uilcanota[FN#38] is a distant land,
Yet, even now, her people come
To range themselves beneath thy law.

[FN#38] The snowy mountain far to the south, in sight from Cuzco.
Uilca, sacred; unuta, water. Here is the source of the river Uilcamayu,
which flows by Ollantay–tampu.

(Ollantay is invested with the fringe. He rises.)

Ollantay.

Urco Huaranca, thee I name
Of Anti–suyu Chief and Lord;
Receive the arrows and the plume,

(Gives them.)

Henceforth thou art our general.
People. Long life to the Mountain Chief.

Ollantay.

Hanco Huayllu,[FN#39] of all my lords
Thou art most venerable and wise,
Being kin to the august High Priest,
It is my wish that thou shouldst give
The ring unto the Mountain Chief.

[FN#39] The aged Hanco Huayllu as Auqui, or Prince of the Blood, and
relation of the High Priest, gave eclat to these ceremonies.

(Urco Huaranca kneels, and Hanco Huayllu addresses him.)

Hanco Huayllu.

This ring around thy finger's placed
That thou mayst feel, and ne'er forget,
That when in fight thou art engaged,
Clemency becomes a hero chief.

Urco Huaranca.

A thousand times, illustrious king,
I bless thee for thy trust in me.

Hanco Huayllu.

Apu Ollantay

Behold the valiant Mountain Chief,
Now fully armed from head to foot,
And bristling like the quiscahuan,[FN#40]
Accoutred as becomes a knight.

[FN#40] Quiscahuan. anything full of thorns.

(Turning to Urco Huaranca.)

Ne'er let thine enemies take thee in rear
Man of the Puna,[FN#41] it ne'er can be said
You fled or trembled as a reed.

[FN#41] Puna, the loftier parts of the Andes.

Urco Huaranca.

Hear me, warriors of the Andes!
Already we have a valiant king,
It might be he will be attacked;
'Tis said th' old Inca sends a force,
The men of Cuzco now advance.
We have not a single day to lose;
Call from the heights our Puna men,
Prepare their arms without delay,
Make Tampu strong with rampart walls,
No outlet leave without a guard;
On hill slopes gather pois'nous herbs
To shoot our arrows, carrying death.

Ollantay (to Urco Huaranca).

Select the chiefs!
Fix all the posts for different tribes;
Our foes keep marching without sleep—
Contrive to check them by surprise.
The compi[FN#42] ruse may cause their flight.

[FN#42] Compi, cloth or a cloak. This was an expression of the ancient
Peruvians, perhaps equivalent to our 'hoodwinking.'

Urco Huaranca.

Thirty thousand brave Antis are here,
Amongst them no weakling is found;
Apu Maruti,[FN#43] the mighty in war,
From high Uilcapampa[FN#44] will come,
On steep Tinquiqueru[FN#45] he'll stand
To march when the signal appears;

[FN#43] Apu Maruti was the head of the ayllu of the Inca Yahuar Huaccac,
grandfather of Pachacuti. It was called the ayllu Aucaylli
Panaca.—Mesa, Anales del Cuzco, quoted by Zegarra.

[FN#44] Uilcapampa, mass of mountains between the Uilcamayu and
Apurimac.

[FN#45] Tinqui Queru, between Urupampa and Tampu. The word means 'two
vases coupled.' Here are two rounded hills connected by a saddle, three
and a half miles from Tampu.

Apu Ollantay

On the opposite side of the stream
Prince Chara[FN#46] has mustered his force;
In the gorge Charamuni[FN#47] I post
Ten thousand armed Antis on watch;
Another such force is in wait
On the left, in the vale of Pachar.[FN#48]
We are ready to meet our foes,
We await them with resolute calm;
They will march in their confident pride
Until their retreat is out off,
Then the trumpet of war shall resound,
From the mountains the stones shall pour down,
Great blocks will be hurled from above.

[FN#46] Chara, was another descendant of Yahuar Huaccac.

[FN#47] A ravine on the right bank of the Vilcamayu.

[FN#48] Pachar is on the left bank of the Vilcamayu opposite
Ollantay–tampu, with which it is connected by a rope bridge.

The Huancas[FN#49] are crushed or dispersed,
Then the knife shall do its fell work,
All will perish by blows from our hands,
Our arrows will follow their flight.

[FN#49] Huancas, natives of the valley of Jauja—Inca recruits.

People and soldiers.

It is well! It is very well!

(Cheers and martial music.)

(Exeunt.)

SCENE 2

A wild place the mountains. Distant view of Ollantay–tampu.

(Enter Rumi–naui, torn and ragged, and covered with blood, with two attendants.)

Rumi–naui.

Ah! Rumi–naui—Rumi–naui,[FN#50]
Thou art a fated rolling stone,[FN#51]
Escaped indeed, but quite alone,
And this is now thy yarahui.

[FN#50] Like Ollantay in his appeal to the Inca, Rumi–naui, in the original Quichua, has recourse to octosyllabic quatrains, the first and last lines rhyming, and the second and third.

[FN#51] Rumi, a stone.

Ollantay posted on the height,
Thou couldst not either fight or see,
Thy men did quickly fall or flee;
No room was there to move or fight.
Thou knowest now thy heart did beat
And flutter like a butterfly;
Thy skill thou couldst not then apply,
No course was left thee but retreat.
They had recourse to a surprise,
Our warriors immolated quite.
Ah! that alone could turn thee white—

63

Apu Ollantay

From shame like that, canst e'er arise?
By thousands did thy warriors fall,
I hardly could alone escape,
With open mouth fell death did gape,
A great disaster did befall.
Holding that traitor to be brave,
I sought to meet him face to face—
Rushing to seek him with my mace,
I nearly found a warrior's grave.
My army then was near the hill,
When suddenly the massive stones
Came crashing down, with cries and moans,
While clarions sounded loud and shrill.
A rain of stones both great and small
Down on the crowd of warriors crashed,
On every side destruction flashed,
Thy heart the slaughter did appal.
Like a strong flood the blood did flow,
Inundating the ravine;
So sad a sight thou ne'er hast seen—
No man survived to strike a blow.
O thou who art by this disgraced,
What figure canst thou ever show
Before the king, who seeks to know
The truth, which must be faced?
'Tis better far myself to kill,
Or losing every scrap of hope,
To hang my body with this rope.

(Takes a sling off his cap—going.)

Yet may it not be useful still?

(Turns again.)

When bold Ollantay's end has come.[FN#52]

64

[FN#52] Clearly, from Rumi–naui's own account, the strategy of Urco Huaranca had been a complete and brilliant success.

(Exit.)

SCENE 3

A garden in the house of the Virgins of the Sun. Chilca shrubs and mulli trees (Schinus Molle) with panicles of red berries. The walls of the house at the back, with a door. A gate (L.) opening on the street.

(YMA SUMAC discovered at the gate looking out. To her enters (R.) PITU SALLA. Both dressed in white with golden belts.)

Pitu Salla.

Yma Sumac, do not approach
So near that gate, and so often;
It might arouse the Mother's wrath.
Thy name, which is so dear to me,
Will surely pass from mouth to mouth.
Honour shall be shown to chosen ones,[FN#53]
Who wish to close the outer gate.

[FN#53] Aclla Cuna, the selected ones, the Virgins of the Sun. They were under the supervision of so called Mothers—Mama Cuna. The novices were not obliged to take the oaths at the end of their novitiate.

Amuse thyself within the walls,
And no one then can say a word.
Think well what you can find within—
It gives you all you can desire,
Of dresses, gold, and dainty food.

Apu Ollantay

Thou art beloved by every one,
E'en Virgins of the royal blood.
The Mothers love to carry thee,
They give thee kisses and caress—
You they prefer to all the rest.
What more could any one desire,
Than always to remain with them,
Destined to be servant of the Sun?
In contemplating Him there's peace.

Yma Sumac.

Pitu Salla, ever you repeat
The same thing and the same advice;
I will open to thee my whole heart,
And say exactly what I think.
Know that to me this court and house
Are insupportable—no less;
The place oppresses—frightens me—
Each day I curse my destiny.
The faces of all the Mama Cuna
Fill me with hatred and disgust,

And from the place they make me sit,
Nothing else is visible.
Around me there is nothing bright,
All are weeping and ne'er cease
If I could ever have my way,
No person should remain within.
I see the people pass outside,
Laughing as they walk along.
The reason it is plain to see—
They are not mewed and cloistered here.
Is it because I have no mother,

That I am kept a prisoner?
Or is it I 'm a rich novice?
Then from to–day I would be poor.
Last night I could not get to sleep,
I wandered down a, garden walk;
In the dead silence of the night,
I heard one mourn. A bitter cry,
As one who sought and prayed for death.
On every side I looked about,
My hair almost on end with fright,
Trembling, I cried, 'Who canst thou be?'
Then the voice murmured these sad words:
'O Sun, release me from this place!'
And this, amidst such sighs and groans!
I searched about, but nothing found—
The grass was rustling in the wind.
I joined my tears to that sad sound,
My heart was torn with trembling fear.
When now the recollection comes,
I'm filled with sorrow and with dread.
You know now why I hate this place.
Speak no more, my dearest friend,
Of reasons for remaining here.

Pitu Salla.

At least go in. The Mother may appear.
Yma Sumac. But pleasant is the light of day.

(Exit, R.)

(Enter MAMA CCACCA, L., in grey with black edges and belt.)

Mama Ccacca.

Pitu Salla, hast thou spoken
All I told thee to that child?

Pitu Salla.

I have said all to her.

Mama Ccacca.

And she, does she answer freely?

Pitu Salla.

She has wept and asked for pity,
Refusing to comply at all.
She will not take the virgin's oath.

Mama Ccacca.

And this in spite of thy advice?

Pitu Salla.

I showed her the dress she will wear,
Telling her misfortune would befall
If she refused to be a chosen one—
That she would ever be an outcast,
And for us a child accursed.

Mama Ccacca.

What can she imagine,
Wretched child of an unknown father,
A maid without a mother,
Just a fluttering butterfly?
Tell her plainly, very plainly,
That these walls offer her a home,
Suited for outcasts such as she,
And here no light is seen.

(Exit, L.)

Pitu Salla.

Ay, my Sumac! Yma Sumac!
These walls will be cruel indeed,
To hide thy surpassing beauty.

(Glancing to where Mama Ccacca went out.)

What a serpent! What a puma!

ACT III

SCENE 1

The Pampa Moroni, a street in Cuzco. Enter RUMI–nAUI (L.)[FN#54] in a long black cloak with a train, and PIQUI CHAQUI (R.), meeting each other.

[FN#54] Rumi–naui is the interlocutor in the Justiniani text, in the Dominican text, and in the text of Spilsbury. Yet Zegarra would substitute the Uillac Uma or High Priest for Rumi–naui. His argument is that the interlocutor was of the blood–royal, and that the High Priest was always of the blood–royal, while Rumi–naui was not. But the text does not say that the interlocutor was of the royal blood. Zegarra also says that the interlocutor wore a black cloak with a long train, and that this was the dress of the High Priest. But it was not the dress of the High Priest as described by the best authorities. It was probably the general mourning dress. The threats addressed to Piqui Chaqui were likely enough to come from a soldier, but not from the High Priest as he is portrayed in this drama.

Rumi–naui.

Whence, Piqui Chaqui, comest thou?
Dost thou here seek Ollantay's fate?

Piqui Chaqui.

Cuzco, great lord, is my birthplace;
I hasten back unto my home.
I care not more to pass my days
In dismal and profound ravines.

Apu Ollantay

Rumi−naui.

Tell me, Ollantay—what does he?

Piqui Chaqui.

He is busy now entangling
An already entangled skein.

Rumi−naui.

What skein?

Piqui Chaqui.

Should you not give me some present
If you want me to talk to you.

Rumi−naui.

With a stick will I give thee blows,
With a rope I will hang thee.

Piqui Chaqui.

Apu Ollantay

O, do not frighten me!

Rumi−naui.

Speak then.

Piqui Chaqui.

Ollantay. Is it Ollantay?
I can remember no more.

Rumi−naui.

Piqui Chaqui! Take care!

Piqui Chaqui.

But you will not listen!
I am turning blind,
My ears are getting deaf,
My grandmother is dead,
My mother is left alone.

Rumi−naui.

Apu Ollantay

Where is Ollantay? Tell me.

Piqui Chaqui.

I am in want of bread,
And the Paccays[FN#55] are not ripe.
I have a long journey to–day—
The desert is very far off.

[FN#55] Paccay (mimosa incana), a tree with large pods, having a
snow–white woolly substance round the seeds, with sweet juice.

Rumi–naui.

If you continue to vex me
I will take your life.

Piqui Chaqui.

Ollantay, is it? He is at work.

Ollantay! He is building a wall,
With very small stones indeed;
They are brought by little dwarfs—
So small that to be a man's size
They have to climb on each other's backs.
But tell me, O friend of the King,[FN#56]

Apu Ollantay

Why art thou in such long clothes,
Trailing like the wings of a sick bird[FN#57]—
As they are black it is better.

[FN#56] The Zegarra and Spilsbury texts have Ccan Incacri, which Zegarra
translates, 'relation of the Inca, of the royal family.' Spilsbury is
more correct. He has 'partisan of the Inca.' The more authentic
Justiniani text has Ccan Pana. The particle ri is one of emphasis or
repetition. It does not mean a relation.

[FN#57] The Zegarra and Spilsbury texts have hualpa, a game bird. The
Justiniani text has anca, an eagle, which is the correct reading.

Rumi–naui.

Hast thou not seen already
That Cuzco is plunged in grief?
The great Inca Pachacuti[FN#58] is dead,
All the people are in mourning,
Every soul is shedding tears.

[FN#58] The Inca Pachacuti does not appear to advantage in the drama.
But he was the greatest man of his dynasty, indeed the greatest that the
red race has produced. He was a hero in his youth, a most able
administrator in mature age. As a very old man some needless cruelties
are reported of him which annoyed his son.

Piqui Chaqui.

Who, then, succeeds to the place

74

Which Pachacuti has left vacant?
If Tupac Yupanqui succeeds,
That Prince is the youngest
There are some others older.[FN#59]

[FN#59] The eldest son was Amaru Tupac. He was passed over by his
father with his own consent, and was ever faithful to his younger
brother. He was an able general.

Rumi−naui.

All Cuzco has elected him,
For the late king chose him,
Giving him the royal fringe;
We could elect no other.

Piqui Chaqui.

I hasten to bring my bed here.[FN#60]

[FN#60] This was exactly what Piqui Chaqui was sent to Cuzco to find
out. The expression Apumusac pununayta, 'I go to fetch my bed,' is one
of joy at any fortunate event, in Quichua.

(Exit running.)

SCENE 2

Great hall of the palace of Tupac Yupanqui. The INCA seated on golden tiana (C.).

(Enter the HIGH PRIEST or UILLAC UMA, with priests and chosen Virgins of
the Sun. The INCA dressed as his father. Uillac Uma in full dress,
wearing the huampar chucu. Virgins in white with gold belts and diadems.
They range themselves by the throne (L.). Then enter RUMI–NAUI and a
crowd of chiefs, all in full dress, ranging themselves by the throne
(R.).)

Tupac Yupanqui.

This day, O Councillors and Chiefs,
Let all receive my benison;
You Holy Virgins of the Sun[FN#61]
Receive our father's tenderest care.

The realm, rejoicing, hails me king;
From deep recesses of my heart
I swear to seek the good of all.

[FN#61] Intic Huamin Caccunan (Intic Huarminca Caycuna, correct), 'Ye
women of the Sun.' Zegarra thought, on the authority of Garcilasso de la
Vega, that these could not be select Virgins of the Sun, because the
virgins were never allowed outside their convent, and not even women
might enter. He is clearly wrong. Much higher authorities than
Garcilasso, as regards this point, especially Valera, tell us that the
virgins were treated with the greatest honour and respect. They took
part in great receptions and festivals, and when they passed along the
streets they had a guard of honour.

Uillac Uma.

Apu Ollantay

To–day the smoke of many beasts
Ascends on high towards the sun,
The Deity with joy accepts
The sacrifice of prayer and praise.
We found in ashes of the birds
Our only Inca, King, and Lord,
In the great llama sacrifice;
All there beheld an eagle's form,
We opened it for augury,
But lo! the heart and entrails gone.
The eagle Anti–suyu means—
To thy allegiance they return.

(Bowing to the Inca.)

Thus I, thy augur, prophesy.

(Acclamation.) (Exeunt all but Uillac Uma and Rumi–naui.)

Tupac Yupanqui (turning to Rumi–naui).

Behold the Hanan–suyu Chief
Who let the enemy escape,
Who led to almost certain death
So many thousands of my men.

Rumi–naui.

Before his death thy father knew
Disaster had befallen me;
'Tis true, O King, it was my fault,

Like a stone[FN#62] I gave my orders,
And volleying stones soon beat me down;
It was with stones I had to fight,
And in the end they crushed my men.
Oh! grant me, Lord, a single chance,
Give perfect freedom to my plans,
Myself will to the fortress march,
And I will leave it desolate.

[FN#62] Rumi. He keeps playing upon his name.

Tupac Yupanqui.

For thee to strive with all thy might,
For thee thine honour to regain,
For thou shalt ne'er command my men
Unless thy worthiness is proved.

Uillac Uma.

Not many days shall pass, O King,
E'er all the Antis are subdued.
I've seen it in the quipu roll,
Haste! Haste! thou Rumi Tunqui. [FN#63]

[FN#63] Again playing upon the name of Rumi−naui. The High Priest calls
for haste, so he substitutes Tunqui for naui (eye), the tunqui (Rupicola
Peruviana) being one of the most beautiful birds in the forests.

(Exeunt.)

SCENE 3

The great terrace entrance to Ollantay–tampu. On R. a long masonry wall
with recesses at intervals. At back a great entrance doorway. On L.
terraces descend, with view of valley and mountains.

(Guards discovered at entrance doorway. To them enter RUMI–NAUI in rags,
his face cut and slashed with wounds, and covered with blood.)

Rumi–naui.

Will no one here have pity on me?
One of the Guards. Who art thou, man?
Who has ill–treated thee?
Thou comest in a frightful state,
Covered with blood and gaping wounds.

Rumi–naui.

Go quickly to thy king and say
That one he loves has come to him.
One of the Guards. Thy name?

Rumi–naui.

There is no need to give a name.
One of the Guards. Wait here.

(Exit one of the guards.)

Apu Ollantay

(Enter OLLANTAY with guards, R. front.)

Rumi–naui.

A thousand times I thee salute,
Ollantay, great and puissant king!
Have pity on a fugitive
Who seeks a refuge here with thee.

Ollantay.

Who art thou, man? Approach nearer.
Who has thus ill–treated thee?
Were such deep and fearful wounds
Caused by a fall, or what mishap?

Rumi–naui.

Thou knowest me, O mighty chief.
I am that stone that fell down once,
But now I fall before thy feet;
O Inca! mercy! Raise me up!

(Kneels.)

Ollantay.

Art thou the noble Rumi–naui,

Great Chief and Lord of Hanan–suyu?

Rumi–naui.

Yes, I was that well–known Chief—
A bleeding fugitive to–day.
Ollantay. Rise, comrade mine. Let us embrace.

(Rises.)

Who has dared to treat thee thus,
And who has brought thee here to me
Within my fortress, on my hearth?

(To attendants.)

Bring new clothes for my oldest friend.

(Exit an attendant.)

How is it that thou art alone?
Camest thou not fearing death?

Rumi–naui.

A new king reigns in Cuzco now—
Tupac Yupanqui is installed.
Against the universal wish,
He rose upon a wave of blood;
Safety he sees in headless trunks,
The sunchu[FN#64] and the nucchu[FN#65] red
Are sent to all he would destroy.

81

Apu Ollantay

[FN#64] Sunchu, a very large composita with a yellow flower, growing round Cuzco. It was one of those which were used on sacred festivals.

[FN#65] Nucchu is a salvia, also considered sacred. A red flower. Perhaps these flowers were sent as a summons from the Inca, but I have not seen the custom mentioned elsewhere.

Doubtless you have not forgot
That I was Hanan–suyu's Chief.
Yupanqui ordered me to come;
Arrived, I came before the king,
And as he has a cruel heart,
He had me wounded as you see;
And now thou knowest, king and friend,
How this new Inca treated me.

Ollantay.

Grieve not, old friend Rumi–naui,
Thy wounds before all must be cured;
I see in thee th' avenging knife,
To use against the tyrant's heart.
At Tampu now we celebrate
The Sun's great Raymi festival;
On that day all who love my name,
Throughout my realms hold festival.

Rumi–naui.

Those three days of festival

To me will be a time of joy,
Perhaps I may be healed by then,
So that my heart may pleasure seek.

Ollantay.

It will be so. For three whole nights
We drink and feast, to praise the Sun,
The better to cast all care aside
We shall be shut in Tampu fort.

Rumi–naui.

The youths, as is their wont, will find
Their great delight in those three nights,
Then will they rest from all their toils,
And carry off the willing girls.

SCENE 4

A corridor in the palace of Chosen Virgins.

(Enter YMA SUMAC and PITU SALLA.)

Yma Sumac.

Pitu Salla, beloved friend,
How long wilt thou conceal from me
The secret that I long to know?

Think, dearest, of my anxious heart,
How I shall be in constant grief
Until you tell the truth to me.
Within these hard and cruel bounds
Does some one suffer for my sins?
My sweet companion, do not hide
From me, who 'tis that mourns and weeps
Somewhere within the garden walls.
How is it she is so concealed
That I can never find the place?

Pitu Salla.

My Sumac, now I'll tell thee all—
Only concerning what you hear,
And still more surely what you see,
You must be dumb as any stone;
And you too must be well prepared
For a most sad heart–rending sight—
'Twill make thee weep for many days.

Yma Sumac.

I will not tell a living soul
What you divulge. But tell me all,
I'll shut it closely in my heart.

SCENE 5

A secluded part of the gardens of the Virgins, (L.) flowers, (R.) a thicket of mulli[FN#66] and chilca,[FN#67] concealing a stone door.

[FN#66] Schineus Molle, a tree with pinnate leaves, and panicles of red berries, well known in the Mediterranean countries, into which it was introduced from Peru. Called by the English 'pepper tree.'

[FN#67] Several bushes are called chilca in Peru. Eupatorium chilca (R. P.), baccharis scandens, and molina latifolia. Stereoxylon pendulum is called puna chilca.

(PITU SALLA and YMA SUMAC.)

Pitu Salla.

In this garden is a door of stone,
But wait until the Mothers sleep,
The night comes on. Wait here for me.

(Exit.)

(Yma Sumac reclines on a bank and sleeps. Night comes on, Yma Sumac awakes.)

Yma Sumac.

A thousand strange presentiments
Crowd on me now, I scarce know what—
Perhaps I shall see that mournful one
Whose fate already breaks my heart.

(Pitu Salla returns with a cup of water, a small covered vase containing food, and a torch which she gives to Yma Sumac. She leads Yma Sumac through bushes to the stone door, fixes the torch, presses something, and the door swings round.)

(CUSI COYLLUR is discovered senseless, extended on the ground, a snake twining itself round her waist.)

Pitu Salla.

Behold the princess for whom you seek.
Well! is thy heart now satisfied?

Yma Sumac.

Oh, my friend, what do I behold?
Is it a corpse that I must see?
Oh, horror! A dungeon for the dead!

(She faints.)

Pitu Salla.

What misfortune has now arrived?
O my Sumac, my dearest love,
O come to thyself without delay!
Arouse thee. Arise, my lovely flower.

(Yma Sumac revives.)

Fear not, my dove, my lovely friend,
'Tis not a corpse. The princess lives,

Unhappy, forlorn, she lingers here.

Yma Sumac.

Is she, then, still a living being?

Pitu Salla.

Approach nearer, and you can help.
She lives indeed. Look. Watch her now.
Give me the water and the food.

(To Cusi Coyllur, while helping her to sit up.)

O fair princess, I bring thee food
And cooling water to refresh.
Try to sit up. I come with help.

Yma Sumac.

Who art thou, my sweetest dove?
Why art thou shut in such a place?

Pitu Salla.

Take a little food, we pray.
Perchance without it, you may die.

Apu Ollantay

Cusi Coyllur.

How happy am I now to see,
After these long and dismal years,
The new and lovely face of one
Who comes with thee and gives me joy.

 Yma Sumac.

O my princess, my sister dear,
Sweet bird, with bosom of pure gold,
What crime can they accuse thee of,
That they can make thee suffer thus?
What cruel fate has placed thee here
With death on watch in serpent's form?

Cusi Coyllur.

O charming child, the seed of love,
Sweet flower for my broken heart,
I have been thrust in this abyss.
I once was joined to a man
As pupil is part of the eye;
But alas! has he forgotten me?
The King know not that we were joined
By such indissoluble bonds,
And when he came to ask my hand,
That King dismissed him in a rage,
And cruelly confined me here.
Many years have passed since then,

Apu Ollantay

Yet, as you see, I'm still alive;
No single soul have I beheld
For all those sad and dismal years,
Nor have I found relief nor hope.
But who art thou, my dear, my love,
So young, so fresh, so pitiful?

Yma Sumac.

I too, like thee, am full of grief,
For long I've wished to see and love,
My poor forlorn and sad princess.
No father, no mother are mine,
And there are none to care for me.

Cusi Coyllur.

What age art thou?

Yma Sumac.

I ought to number many years,
For I detest this dreadful house,
And as it is a dreary place,
The time in it seems very long.

Pitu Salla.

She ought to number just ten years
According to the account I've kept.

Cusi Coyllur.

 And what is thy name?

Yma Sumac.

They call me Yma Sumac now,
But to give it me is a mistake.

Cusi Coyllur.

O my daughter! O my lost love,
Come to thy mother's yearning heart.

(Embraces Yma Sumac.)

Thou art all my happiness,
My daughter, come, O come to me;
This joy quite inundates my soul,
It is the name I gave to thee.

Yma Sumac.

O my mother, to find thee thus!

We must be parted never more.
Do not abandon me in grief.
To whom can I turn to free thee,
To whom can I appeal for right?

Pitu Salla.

Make no noise, my dearest friend.:
To find us thus would ruin me.
Let us go. I fear the Mothers.

Yma Sumac (to Cusi Coyllur).

Suffer a short time longer here,
Until I come to take thee hence,
Patience for a few more days.
Alas! my mother dear! I go,
But full of love, to seek for help.

(Exeunt closing the stone door, all but Cusi Coyllur. They extinguish the torch.)

SCENE 6

Great hall in the palace of Tupac Yupanqui.

(The INCA discovered seated on the tiana. To him enter the UILLAC UMA, in full dress.)

Apu Ollantay

Tupac Yupanqui.

I greet thee, great and noble Priest!
Hast thou no news of Rumi−naui.

Uillac Uma.

Last night, with guards, I wandered out
On heights towards Uilcanuta.
Far off I saw a crowd in chains,
No doubt the Anti prisoners,
For they are all defeated quite.
The cacti[FN#68] on the mountains smoke,
E'en now the fortress is in flames.

[FN#68] A kind of cactus, of which they make needles, grows abundantly
on the mountains round Ollantay−tampu. It is called ahuarancu. They set
fire to the cacti as a war signal. Zegarra calls it a thistle. The word
in the Justiniani text is ahuarancu.

Tupac Yupanqui.

And Ollantay, is he taken?
Perhaps—I hope his life is saved.

Uillac Uma.

Ollantay was among the flames,

92

'Tis said that no one has escaped.

Tupac Yupanqui.

The Sun, my Father, is my shield,
I am my father's chosen child.
We must subdue the rebel host,
For that I am appointed here.

(Enter a CHASQUI with a quipu in his hand.)

The Chasqui.

This morning at the dawn of day,
Rumi−naui despatched this quipu.

Tupac Yupanqui (to the Uillac Uma).

See what it says.

Uillac Uma.

This knot, coloured burnt ahuarancu,
Tells us that Tampu too is burnt;
This triple knot to which is hung
Another which is quintuple,
In all of quintuples are three,
Denotes that Anti−suyu's thine,

93

Its ruler prisoner of war.

Tupac Yupanqui (to the Chasqui).

And thou. Where wert thou?

The Chasqui.

Sole King and Lord! Child of the Sun!
I am the first to bring the news,
That thou mayst trample on the foe,
And in thine anger drink their blood.

Tupac Yupanqui.

Did I not reiterate commands
To spare and not to shed their blood—
Not anger but pity is my rule.

The Chasqui.

O Lord, we have not shed their blood;
They were all captured in the night,
Unable to resist our force.

Tupac Yupanqui.

Apu Ollantay

Recount to me in full detail
The circumstances of the war.

The Chasqui.

For a signal thy warriors wait.
The nights passed at Tinquiqueru,[FN#69]
Concealed in the cavern below,
Yanahuara[FN#70] men joining us late.
We waited within the large cave,
Thy men always ready to fight,
Behind foliage well out of sight,
Thy warriors patient and brave.

[FN#69] Tinqui Queru, between Urupampa and Tampu. The word means 'two
vases coupled.' Here are two rounded hills connected by a saddle, three
and a half miles from Tampu. [Taken from FN#45.]

[FN#70] Yanahuara, a ravine near Urubamba, where some of the troops of
Rumi–naui had been posted.

But for three long days and dark nights,
No food for the zealous and bold;
Feeling hungry, thirsty, and cold,
We waited and watched for the lights.[FN#71]
Rumi–naui sent orders at length,
When the Raymi[FN#72] they carelessly keep,
And all of them drunk or asleep,
We were then to rush on with our strength.
Word came to surprise our foes,
Rumi–naui had opened the gate,

Apu Ollantay

As cautious and silent as fate—
We were masters with none to oppose.

[FN#71] Signal lights.

[FN#72] Ccapac Raymi, the great festival of the Sun. December 22.

Those rebels fell into the trap,
The arrows came on them like rain,
Most died in their sleep without pain,
Not knowing their fatal mishap.
Ollantay, still trusting, was ta'en,
The same Urco Huaranca befell;
Hanco Huayllu is captive as well,
We thy rebels in fetters detain.
The Antis by thousands are slain,
A fearful example is made,
They are beaten, crushed, and betrayed,
Their women in sorrow and pain.

Tupac Yupanqui.

As witness of what has occurred,
On Vilcamayu's storied banks,
No doubt thou hast told me the truth.
It was a well designed attack.

(Enter RUMI−nAUI followed by several chiefs.)

Rumi−naui.

96

Apu Ollantay

Great Inca, I kneel at thy feet,
This time You will hear my report,
I beseech thee to deign to restore
The trust that I forfeited once.

(Kneels.)

Tupac Yupanqui.

Rise, great Chief, receive my regard,
I accept thy great service with joy;
Thou didst cast o'er the waters. thy net,

And hast captured a marvellous fish.

Rumi−naui.

Our enemies perished in crowds,
Their chiefs were captured and bound,
Overwhelmed by my terrible force,
Like a rook detached from the heights.

Tupac Yupanqui.

Was much blood shed in the assault?

Rumi−naui.

Apu Ollantay

No, Lord, not a drop has been shed,
To thine orders I strictly adhered.
Those Antis were strangled in sleep,
But the fort is entirely razed.

Tupac Yupanqui.

Where are the rebels?

Rumi−naui.

They are waiting with agonised fear,
For their fate, to perish by cords.
The people are sending up cries,
Demanding their deaths without fail.
Their women are now in their midst,
The children raise hideous cries;
It is well that thine order should pass
To finish their traitorous lives.

Tupac Yupanqui.

It must be so without any doubt,
That the orphans may not be alone,
Let all perish, not sparing one,
Thus Cuzco recovers her peace,
Let the traitors be brought before me.
In my presence the sentence they'll hear.

Apu Ollantay

(Exit Rumi−naui, and re−enter followed by guards in charge of OLLANTAY,
URCO HUARANCA, and HANCO HAUYLLU, bound and blindfold, followed by
guards
with PIQUI CHAQUI bound.)

Tupac Yupanqui.

Take the bands off the eyes of those men.
And now, Ollantay, where art thou?
And where art thou, O Mountain Chief?
Soon thou wilt roll down from the heights.

(To the soldiers who bring in Piqui Chaqui.)

Whom have we here?

Piqui Chaqui.

Many fleas in the Yuncas abound,
And torment the people full sore,
With boiling water they are killed,
And I, poor flea,[FN#73] must also die.

[FN#73] Piqui Chaqui is literally 'flea foot.' He is punning on his
name.

Tupac Yupanqui.

Tell me, Hanco Huayllu, tell me,
Why art thou Ollantay's man?

Did not my father honour thee?
Did he not grant thy requests?
Did he ever have a secret from thee?
Speak also, you, the other rebels,
Ollantay and the Mountain Chief.

Ollantay.

O father, we have nought to say,
Our crimes are overwhelming us.

Tupac Yupanqui (to the Uillac Uma).

Pronounce their sentence, great High Priest.

Uillac Uma.

The light that fills me from the Sun
Brings mercy and pardon to my heart.

Tupac Yupanqui.

Now thy sentence, Rumi–naui.

Rumi–naui.

For crimes enormous such as these
Death should ever be the doom
It is the only way, O King!
To warn all others from such guilt.
To stout tocarpus[FN#74] they should be
Secured and bound with toughest rope,
Then should the warriors freely shoot
Their arrows until death is caused.

[FN#74] Tocarpu, a pole or stake used at executions. Condemned prisoners were fastened to a tocarpu before being hurled over a precipice.

Piqui Chaqui.

Must it be that evermore
The Antis must all perish thus?
Alas! then let the branches burn
What pouring out of blood is here.[FN#75]

Rumi–naui.

Silence, rash man, nor dare to speak,

[FN#75] Piqui Chaqui had an inkling that the Inca had expressed dislike at the shedding of blood. He ventured to say these words in the faint hope that they might remind the Inca of this dislike.

(General lamentation outside.)

Having been rolled just like a stone,
My heart has now become a stone.[FN#76]

[FN#76] Rumi−naui at it again: for ever ringing changes on his name
rumi, a stone.

Tupac Yupanqui.

Know that tocarpus are prepared.
Remove those traitors from my sight,
Let them all perish, and at once.

Rumi−naui.

Take these three men without delay
To the dreaded execution stakes;
Secure them with unyielding ropes,
And hurl them from the lofty rocks.

Tupac Yupanqui.

Stop! Cast off their bonds.

(The guards unbind them. They all kneel.)

(To Ollantay, kneeling).

Rise from thy knees; come to my side.

Apu Ollantay

(Rises.)

Now thou hast seen death very near,
You that have shown ingratitude,
Learn how mercy flows from my heart;
I will raise thee higher than before.
Thou wert Chief of Anti−suyu,
Now see how far my love will go;
I make thee Chief in permanence.
Receive this plume[FN#77] as general,
This arrow[FN#77] emblem of command.[FN#78]

[FN#77] The plume and the arrow were the insignia of a general.

[FN#78] Rather a staggerer for Rumi−naui! Perhaps, too, the change is
too sudden, and infringes the probabilities. Tupac Yupanqui may have
thought that his father had been unjust and that there were excuses. It
is known that the young Inca was indignant at some other cruelties of his
father. As a magnanimous warrior he may have despised the treacherous
methods of Rumi−naui. He may have valued Ollantay's known valour and
ability, and have been loth to lose his services. All these
considerations may have influenced him more or less. The rebels were the
best men he had.

Tupac Yupanqui (to the Uillac Uma).

Thou mighty Pontiff of the Sun,
Robe him in the regal dress.
Raise up the others from their knees,
And free them from the doom of death.

Apu Ollantay

(Urco Huaranca, Hanco Huayllu, and Piqui Chaqui rise, the latter looking much relieved. The Uillac Uma places the robe on Ollantay's shoulders.)

Uillac Uma.

Ollantay, learn to recognise
Tupac Yupanqui's generous mind;
From this day forth be thou his friend,
And bless his magnanimity.
This ring contains my potent charm,
For this I place it on thy hand.

(Gives him a ring, or bracelet.)

This mace receive, 'tis from the king,

(Gives him a mace (champi).)

It is his gracious gift to thee.

Ollantay.

With tears I shall nearly consume
That mace thus presented to me;
I am tenfold the great Inca's slave,
In this world no equal is found,
My heart's fibres his latchets shall be;
From this moment my body and soul
To his service alone shall belong.

Tupac Yupanqui.

Apu Ollantay

Now, Mountain Chief! come near to me,
Ollantay is given the arrow and plume,
Though to me he gave fury and war.
Notwithstanding all that has passed
He continues the Andean chief,
And will lead his rebels to peace;
Thee also I choose for the plume;
From this day thou art a great chief,
And never forget in thy thoughts,
I saved thee from death and disgrace.

Urco Huaranca.

Great King and most merciful Lord,
But now, expecting my death,
I am ever thy most faithful slave.

(Uillac Uma gives him the plume and arrow.)

Uillac Uma.

O Urco, the Inca has made
A great and a powerful chief,
And grants thee with marvellous grace
The arrow and also the plume.

Rumi−naui.

Illustrious King, I venture to ask,

Apu Ollantay

Will Anti−suyu have two chiefs.

Tupac Yupanqui.

There will not be two, O Rumi−naui
The Mountain Chief will rule the Antis;
In Cuzco Ollantay will reign—
As Viceroy deputed by me
His duties will call him to act
As ruler throughout the whole realm.

Ollantay.

O King! thou dost raise me too high,
A man without service or claim;
I am thy obedient slave—
Mayst thou live for a thousand years.

Tupac Yupanqui.

The mascapaycha now bring forth,
And to it the llautu attach.
Uillac Uma, adorn him with these,
And proclaim his state to the world.
Yes, Ollantay shall stand in my place,
Raised up like the star of the morn,
For Colla this month I shall start;
All preparations are made.
In Cuzco Ollantay will stay,
My Ranti[FN#79] and Viceroy and friend.

[FN#79] Ranti, a deputy.

Ollantay.

I would fain, O magnanimous King,
Follow thee in the Chayanta war;
Thou knowest my love for such work.
Peaceful Cuzco is not to my taste,
I prefer to be thy Canari,[FN#80]
To march in the van of thy force,
And not to be left in the rear.

[FN#80] Canari, a warlike tribe of Indians, in the south part of the
kingdom of Quito. They were first conquered by Tupac Yupanqui, and they
became devoted to him.

Tupac Yupanqui.

Thou shouldst find the wife of thy choice,
And with her reign happily here
In Cuzco; repose without care;
Rest here while I'm absent in war.

Ollantay.

Great King, thy sorrowful slave
Already had chosen a wife.

Tupac Yupanqui.

Apu Ollantay

How is it I know not of this?
It should be reported to me.
I will load her with suitable gifts;
Why was this concealed from my eyes?

Ollantay.

In Cuzco itself disappeared
That sweet and adorable dove;
One day she did rest in my arms,
And the next no more to be seen.
In grief I made search far and near,
Earth seemed to have swallowed her up,
To have buried her far from my sight;
O such, mighty King, is my grief.

Tupac Yupanqui.

Ollantay! afflict not thyself,
For now thou must take up thy place
Without turning thy eyes from thy work.

(To Uillac Uma.)

High priest, obey my command.

(The Uillac Uma goes to the wings (R.) and addresses the people outside.)

Uillac Uma.

Apu Ollantay

O people, hear what I say:
The Inca, our King and our Lord,
Thus declares his imperial will:
Ollantay shall reign in his place.

People outside.

Ollantay Ranti! Ollantay Ranti!

(Shouts and acclamations.)

Tupac Yupanqui (to Rumi–naui and other chiefs.)

You also render him homage.

Rumi–naui.

Prince Ollantay! Incap Ranti!
Thy promotion gives me joy.
All the Antis now released,
Return rejoicing to their homes.

(He and all the Chiefs bow to Ollantay.)

Guards without.

You cannot pass. Go back! go back!

Voice without. Why, is this a festive day?
Let me pass. I must see the king;
I pray you do not stop me,
Do not drive me from the door;
If you stop me I shall die.
Have a care. You will kill me.

Tupac Yupanqui.

What noise is that without?

Guard.

It is a young girl who comes weeping
And insists upon seeing the king.

Tupac Yupanqui.

Let her come in.

(Enter Yma Sumac.)

Yma Sumac.

Which is the Inca, my lord,
That I may kneel down at his feet?

Apu Ollantay

Uillac Uma.

Who art thou, charming maid?
Behold the King.

(Yma Sumac throws herself at the King's feet.)

Yma Sumac. O my King! be thou my father,
Snatch from evil thy poor servant.
Extend thy royal hand to me.
O merciful child of the Sun,
My mother is dying at this hour
In a foul and loathsome cave;
She is killed in cruel martyrdom—
Alas I she is bathed in her own blood.

Tupac Yupanqui.

What inhumanity, poor child!
Ollantay, take this case in hand.

Ollantay.

Young maiden, take me quickly there;
We will see who it is that suffers.

Yma Sumac.

No, sir. Not so. It is the King himself
Should go with me.
Perhaps he may recognise her;

(To Ollantay.)

For you, I know not who you are.
O King, arise, do not delay,
I fear my mother breathes her last,
At least may be in mortal pain;
O Inca! Father! grant my prayer.

Uillac Uma.

Illustrious King, thou wilt consent;
Let us all seek this luckless one—
Thou canst release from cruel bonds.
Lot us go, O King!

Tupac Yupanqui (rising).

Come all! Come all!
In midst of reconciliations
This young maid assaults my heart.

(Exeunt.)

SCENE 7

The garden in the palace of Virgins of the Sun (same scene as Act III,

Scene 5). Stone door more visible.

(Enter the INCA TUPAC YUPANQUI with YMA SUMAC, OLLANTAY, UILLAC UMA and
RUMI nAUI; URCO HUARANCA, HANCO HUAYLLU and PIQUI CHAQUI in the background.)

Tupac Yupanqui.

But this is the Aclla Huasi;[FN#81]
My child, art thou not mistaken?
Where is thy imprisoned mother?

[FN#81] Aclla, chosen; Huasi, house: palace of the Virgins of the sun.

Yma Sumac.

In a dungeon within these bounds
My mother has suffered for years,
Perhaps even now she is dead.

(She points to the stone door.)

Tupac Yupanqui.

What door is this?

(Enter MAMA CCACCA and PITU SALLA. Mama Ccacca kneels and kisses the Inca's hand.)

Apu Ollantay

Mama Ccacca.

Is it a dream or reality,
That I behold my sovereign?
Tupac Yupanqui. Open that door.

(Mama Ccacca opens the door.)

(CUSI COYLLUR discovered chained and fainting, with a puma and a snake,
one on each side of her.)

Yma Sumac.

O my mother, I feared to find
That you had already passed away;
Pitu Salla! Haste. Bring water.
Perhaps my dove may still revive.

(Exit Pitu Salla.)

Tupac Yupanqui.

What horrid cavern do I see?
Who is this woman? what means it?
What cruel wretch thus tortures her?
What means that chain bound around her?
Mama Ccacca, come near to me
What hast thou to say to this?
Is it the effect of malice
That this poor creature lingers here?

Mama Ccacca.

It was thy father's dread command;
A punishment for lawless love.

Tupac Yupanqui.

Begone! begone! harder than rock.[FN#82]
Turn out that puma and the snake,[FN#83]
Break down that door of carved stone.

[FN#82] Ccacca means a rock.

[FN#83] My former translation, and those of Barranca and Tschudi,
treated puma and amaru (snake) as epithets applied to Mama Ccacca.
Zegarra considers that the puma and snake were intended to be actually in
the dungeon, and I believe he is right. The puma would not have hurt his
fellow−prisoner. Unpleasant animals were occasionally put into the
prisons of criminals. The Incas kept pumas as pets.

(To Mama Ccacca.)

Let me not see thy face again.
A woman living as a bat;
This child has brought it all to light.

(Enter Pitu Salla with water. She sprinkles it over Cusi Coyllur, who
revives.)

Apu Ollantay

Cusi Coyllur.

Where am I? who are these people?
Yma Sumac, my beloved child,
Come to me, my most precious dove.
Who are all these men before me?

(She begins to faint again and is restored by water.)

Yma Sumac.

Fear not, my mother, 'tis the King;
The King himself comes to see you.
The great Yupanqui is now here.
Speak to him. Awake from thy trance.

Tupac Yupanqui.

My heart is torn and sorrowful
At sight of so much misery.
Who art thou, my poor sufferer?
Child, tell me now thy mother's name?

Yma Sumac.

Father! Inca! Clement Prince!
Have those cruel bonds removed.

The Uillac Uma.

It is for me to remove them,
And to relieve this sore distress.

(Cuts the rope fastening Cusi Coyllur to the wall.)

Ollantay (to Yma Sumac).

What is thy mother's name?

Yma Sumac.

Her name was once Cusi Coyllur,
But it seems a mistake. Her joy
Was gone when she was prisoned here.

Ollantay.

O renowned King, great Yupanqui,
In her you see my long lost wife.

(Prostrates himself before the Inca.)

Tupac Yupanqui.

Apu Ollantay

It all appears a dream to me.
The 'Star'! my sister![FN#84] and thy wife.
O sister! what newly found joy.
O Cusi Coyllur, my sister,
Come here to me, and embrace me,
Now thou art delivered from woe.

[FN#84] The early Incas never married their sisters or relations.
Pachacuti's mother was daughter of the chief of Anta. His wife,
Anahuarqui, was no relation. But the wife of Tupac Yupanqui was his
sister Mama Ocllo.

(Music.)

Thou hast found thy loving brother;
Joy calms the anguish of my heart.

(Embraces Cusi Coyllur.)

Cusi Coyllur.

Alas! my brother, now you know
The cruel tortures I endured
During those years of agony;
Thy compassion now has saved me.

Tupac Yupanqui.

Who art thou, dove, that hast suffered?
For what sin were you prisoned here?
Thou mightest have lost thy reason.

Thy face is worn, thy beauty gone,
Thy looks as one risen from death.

Ollantay.

Cusi Coyllur, I had lost thee,
Thou wast quite hidden from my sight,
But thou art brought again to life—
Thy father should have killed us both.
My whole heart is torn with sorrow.
Star of joy, where is now thy joy?
Where now thy beauty as a star?
Art thou under thy father's curse?

Cusi Coyllur.

Ollantay, for ten dreary years
That dungeon has kept us apart;
But now, united for new life,
Some happiness may yet be ours.
Yupanqui makes joy succeed grief,
He may well count[FN#85] for many years.

[FN#85] A play upon the word yupanqui, which means literally, 'you will count.' The word was a title of the Incas, meaning, 'you will count as virtuous, brave,' &c.

Uillac Uma.

Bring new robes to dress the princess.

Apu Ollantay

(They put on her royal robes. The High Priest kisses her hand.)

Tupac Yupanqui.

Ollantay, behold thy royal wife,
Honour and cherish her henceforth.
And thou, Yma Sumac, come to me,
I enlace you in the thread of love;
Thou art the pure essence of Coyllur.

(Embraces her.)

Ollantay.

Thou art our protector, great King,
Thy noble hands disperse our grief;
Thou art our faith and only hope—
Thou workest by virtue's force.

Tupac Yupanqui.

Thy wife is now in thy arms;
All sorrow now should disappear,
Joy, new born, shall take its place.

(Acclamations from the Chiefs, and Piqui Chaqui. Music: huancars
(drums), pincullus (flutes), and pututus (clarions).)

Printed in the United States
52139LVS00004B/135